A FLIGHT TO A THREE-DIMENSIONAL LEGACY

Vanessa S. Brown

A Flight To A Three-Dimensional Legacy by Vanessa Brown

Published by Living Waters Global Publishing

Living Waters Global Publishing

Roebuck, SC 29376

www.lwgpublishing.com

This book or parts thereof may not be reproduced in any form, stored in a retrieval system, or transmitted in any form by any means – electronic, mechanical, photocopy, recording, or otherwise – without prior written permission of the publisher, except as provided by United States of America copyright law.

Scripture quotations marked ESV are from the English Standard Version. Copyright © 2012 by Crossway. Used by permission. All rights reserved.

Scripture quotations marked NIV are from the New International Version. Copyright © 2015 by Holman Bible Publishers. Used by permission.

Scripture quotations marked NKJV are from the New King James Version. Copyright © 1982 by Thomas Nelson. Used by permission.

Scripture quotations marked MSG are from the Message Version. Copyright © 2014 by Eugene Peterson. Used by permission.

Scripture quotations marked AMP are from the Amplified Version. Copyright © 1983 by Zondervan Bible Publishers. Used by permission.

Scripture quotations marked KJV are from the King James Version of the Bible.

Copyright © 2024 Vanessa Brown

All rights reserved.

Cover Design by Living Waters Global Publishing
Visit the author's website at vanessabrownglobal.org/mindsetcoachv

ISBN: 9798987897669

DEDICATION

Thank you, God, for loving me, Fathering me, and pushing me. I owe my life to you. I thank you that I have submitted my life and all my worth to you, for it is you who makes my name great. I love you, sweet Father God, Jesus, and Holy Spirit. This book is unto you.

TABLE OF CONTENTS

Foreword 7
Preface 1
Introduction 1
Section 1 1
   Reserved and weighty 1
      Reserved and Training 4
      Critical Phases of Flight 7
      Devalued Reserves 9
      Reserved and Waiting 12
      Reserved and Weighty Discussion 13

Section 2 15
   The Divine Attitude 15
      Overview and Disclosure of A Flight to A Three-Dimensional Legacy 16
      Fix the Load Imbalances 17
      Maintaining a Divine Attitude 21
      Check Air Filters, Trash, and Lavatories 22
      Are You Ready for an Uncommon Journey? 24
      "Are We Being a Good Steward?" 28
      Divine Attitude Discussion 35

Section 3 39
   Divine Assembly 39
      Divine Building 41
      Cross-Check Analysis 44
      Knowing You and Your Audience 45
      Divine Intervention: We are the Students First 51
      "There is a Necessary Purge!" 51

    The Process 54
    Divine Assembly- Corporate Settings 55
    Grace For the Race 59
    Section 3 - Divine Assembly Questions 61

Section 4 65
  Divine Acceleration 65
    We cannot Dethrone God's Process 70
    Grit Work 72
    The Walk of Sobriety 77
    A Call to the Mount 82
    Divine Acceleration Discussion 85

About The Author 89

FOREWORD

You have just boarded Kingdom Flight. Welcome aboard!

This flight is a first-class flight prepared to take you to your next place. During your travels, you must trust the pilot God with all of your heart and lean not to your own understanding. Continue to acknowledge that He is in control of steering this plane. Please remain in your assigned seat and enjoy the ride of ACCELERATION! Keep in mind you will not be on this flight very long as things are happening very quickly. However, enjoy the ride and the amenities provided to your new place in Him.

It's amazing when God allows you to experience the words written on paper as you are writing them. This reminds me of the scripture that tells us, "Write down the revelation and make it plain on tablets so that a herald may run with it" (Habakkuk 2:2 NIV). A Flight to a Three-Dimensional Legacy is not just a book. It's an experience. I've watched Vanessa go from nothing, having the slightest clue of where God was taking her, to a propelled journey of victory.

During the acceleration process, you must remain in your seat and keep your belt of truth fastened as it is still a little bumpy. Most would perceive that being accelerated is a smooth transition to a higher place. God tells us that to whom much is given, much is required. There is more that God requires of us as we progress and undergo acceleration.

I've learned to be content in all things the famous Apostle Paul said. He then says I can do all things through Christ that strengthens me. The reason Paul's divine attitude is of contentment is because he remains in Christ following the path of Christ, which then, in turn, gives him the strength to embrace and endure all things. Once accelerated, one would think the turbulence is over, when, in essence, it never ends. The famous

David said, "I was glad to be afflicted that I might learn of your ways." Going back to the principle to whom much is given, much is required. The turbulence does not stop. You just develop and mature to a place of contentment in Christ, keeping the belt of truth close and always abounding in the Lord's marvelous works. We must wait on the instruction of the captain who is flying us higher to unfasten our belt of truth to walk and release. God orders the steps of a good man. In this case, God is the captain. God says, "I will establish you and make your name great." So why do we find ourselves trying to make our own name great, establishing a weakened foundation that is so easily moved by the winds and storms of this world?

As you go through the acceleration process there comes a point and time where God prepares you for landing. He notifies you how close you are to reaching the finish line or reaching your next place in Him safely. He reiterates the importance of keeping hold of your belt of truth. When you get closer to your next place, you will have to fasten your belt of truth, so buckle up!

At times, when preparing for landing (Divine Assembly), you may feel like you're going to fall. You may feel like you're going to fail. God says buckle up. I have you in the palm of my hand. I am within you. You will not fail. You may stumble, but I won't let you fall. Greater is He who is in you than he who is of the world.

It is my honor to welcome you to a Flight to a Three-Dimensional Legacy. Please keep your belt of truth fastened as you are now preparing to land in your next.

Aleshia Brown

Aleshia Brown
CEO of Living Waters Global Publishing

PREFACE

"A Flight to A Three-Dimensional Legacy" is to bring foreknowledge, insight, and revival to your life. This book is not to condemn, ostracize, or disrespect no man's walk or quality of life, but it is first to bring honor to all who came before us and learn to shift trajectories from what they may not have been able to grasp or decided not to grasp. Now, because we know better, we can, by all means, extrapolate a greater understanding of the depth, height, and width of building ourselves and others. We will now be able to bless generations to come with a greater formation of thinking that drives actionable results.

For as long as I can remember, I watched immediate family and others who were connected work in subliminal circumstances, and at the end of it all, there was limited influence over what was actually imparted to me and my siblings. I began noticing my siblings and I following the same pattern. We would search for a good-paying job and work someone else's vision to gain a decent paycheck so we could pay our bills on time, come to a borrowed home, and start the same cycle again the next day. This went on until they came of age to receive retirement. They then lived off of partial benefits and pensions. Others repeated the same cycle, except they owned their homes, which will lead me into the next segue after I define a few words that will establish more understanding of this text.

According to Oxford Languages, the word subliminal can be defined as "perceived by or affecting someone's mind without their being aware of it." Circumstance can be defined as "one's state of financial or material welfare." And lastly, the word inheritance can be defined as "a financial term describing the assets passed down to individuals after someone dies. Most inheritances consist of cash that's parked in a bank account but may contain stocks, bonds, cars, jewelry, automobiles, art, antiques, real estate, and other tangible assets."

Proverbs 13:22 AMP says, "*A good man leaves an inheritance to his children's children.*" In the cultural context, it is clear that the passing of stocks, bonds, antiques, real estate, and other tangible assets to one's children and grandchildren would help initiate the segue to creating a legacy. My family worked for a profit to take care of recurring bills and immediate family needs, rather than seeking God to show them where they should put their foot next, to secure and store up real property, assets, and land which would allow us to be introduced to the steps of creating avenues of generational wealth. They knew how to participate in worldly sacrifices that provided them with temporal gifts, which did not necessarily acquire a rightful stance in God but took care of the physical demands of man. From my results, it does not seem that they pressed for a more excellent way, which comes by Godly sacrifices, the extent of more eternal things, that my siblings and I could have acquired a taste to impart for generations to come. I know that they could not teach me because they were not taught fully, and their parents were not fully taught, or they rebelled against the truth about establishing our salvation by faith so we could access our inheritance in God's kingdom. As a result, we perish from a lack of greater knowledge of good living. This means that for decades, and for more than a century, all that was revealed to our next of kin was, "You must work hard for the money." I even remember singing this soundtrack song at a very young and tender age, not knowing it was an early seed being planted inside of me that would later cause a baffled transfer of stewardship that led to no residual profits.

When I looked up the word profit, it explained that it is the difference between the amount earned and the amount spent. When I compare this analogy with the phrase faith without works is dead, I began to think about how much time I have spent wasting my time in world production vs. the undergirding of wisdom production. The word perform can mean to act or a form of entertainment, whereas undergird means we are building a firm foundation.

Now let's deliberate on World Production vs. Wisdom Production. World production is working for the things of this world. Worldly production amounts to humanism, which can be assessed as borderline divination, which I refuse to be a part of. World production means we usually do not have anything that we actually own, whereas if we are using our faith coupled with wisdom production, then the things we gain are not temporal, the things we gain are generational, and in the long-term eternal.

We can work for someone or a company for 50 years and gain a few dollars in pension or retirement income, but what did this world production enhance in our minds, will, intellect, emotions, and spirit? From my experience, not much, just a little anger, misunderstanding, bitterness, rejection, internal and external chaos, minimal feedback, and increased bondage to another person's dream.

Whereas when we focus on wisdom production, we are working on the continuous edification of our spirits and building up of ourselves morally. We are attentive to having good character, which in turn increases favor with God and man, according to Luke 2:52 MSG, "And Jesus matured, growing up in both body and spirit, blessed by both God and people."

We are then able to focus on building our dreams, that have already been placed inside of us by God, to walk out our predestination, callings, and elections. However, we cannot tap into wisdom production, if we cannot center ourselves on God's divine instructions, and hear past what we physically see, smell, taste, feel, and touch.

As a result of our limited views, we can become numb and our lives switch gears to autopilot. We look up, and we have nothing to show for things that we have been loyal by default to, that are the enemies of flesh and pride when we should have been building up ourselves in eternal things. These eternal things that we should build on are called "purpose." See God had a plan and a purpose when he created us, and it had nothing to do with punching clocks every day. Yes, we do go through seasons where we are placed in the marketplace to work, and this is fine, but after so long, we begin to feel invalid, without intention, being succumbed to increased delays and physical, mental, and emotional fatalities.

Before we know it, we look up and our children are grown with their own children, and we are still looking for that great job, or still working for someone else, so we can survive paycheck to paycheck. Good Jobs are great for a purpose, when you have a plan of intent and purpose, do that, but after that, what else are we supposed to do with what we have learned, or tapped into while on these good jobs? Our jobs, if viewed spiritually, are what we call our marketplace ministries. The marketplace is not a bad place to be if we view our jobs as our ministry unto the Lord, and not just collecting a consistent paycheck. When we view our jobs as paychecks, it locks us into the world's money systems, which keeps us working for a paycheck.

Living paycheck to paycheck is not what the LORD desires for his people, and so I do believe this is what he means when he says Faith without works is dead, we get the temporal profits, that can be taken anytime man gets ready, so that leads me back to what are we really building, if we are not building on our Kingdom Bank, which is accepting salvation and the Holy Spirit, and leaning not to our own understanding, but remaining consistent to sow and tithe out of our temporal finances, in order to reap our heavenly inheritance. If we work for 50 years and don't find good ground to sow into, we have given our time and gained worldly things, and in exchange end up losing our soul, then what really have we gained? When we die, we cannot take any of these temporal things, so where does that leave our souls and the family that is left behind, it still leaves our mind, will, emotion, and intellect, bankrupt in the things GOD wants for us.

Such themes of Inheritance and heritage are widely discussed throughout the Bible. To be clear inheritance may refer to tangible items typically being money or real estate. Heritage often refers to things that are intangible typically like beliefs, morals, and ethical standards.

I have matriculated in different realms of training and education throughout my life and in exchange I have received a Ministerial license, a Real Estate license, a provisional teaching license, a Bachelor's Degree, a Master's Degree, and an Associate in Network Security, which increased my foresight, my words, my analytical and supplemental reasoning skills. This training and educational experience also brought another level of understanding, and broad communications, but never have these steps scratched the surface of what the words legacy or heritage meant in word, theme, thought, and/or action. However, I do remember discussing the surface level of beliefs, but from a limited perspective. By limited perspective, I mean the discussion can only be as powerful as the writer is willing to research, explain, characterize, delve, and so forth.

So, I am grateful to even share with you the revelation of my intense preparation that allowed me to leave a heritage on earth by my strong adoption in the kingdom of God. As I am now building my own legacy in hope, faith, and admonishment of the LORD JESUS. Only He sets up and only he sets down, this is the LORD's doing and it is marvelous in HIS eyes. Even with me being well educated and outspoken in general, none of my high school or college educators invited me to study this word legacy or question my heritage. The underlying reason I ran after education and knowledge is that I told myself I would not perish from lack of a culminated vision with the unadulterated truth and that I would protect myself from having a poor depth of knowledge; however, it was not me furthering the secondary education that propelled me into this unadulterated, comprehensive truth. It takes a fully yielded vessel with the want to change and turn into a different path. Through time I was able to increase my yielding to the Holy Spirit. It takes partnership with the Holy Spirit and a continuous yes, sometimes daily yes, to ascend to your rightful place in the kingdom.

God is a gentleman, and so are Jesus and the Holy Spirit. Nothing will be wasted or forced upon you. It took 20 years of doing it my own way to fully understand that no amount of education or studying the world's wisdom will set you right with God.

Most people believe it comes by osmosis and your relationship with the Holy Spirit, but it does not, and it does not come like a microwave either. Oxford Language defines osmosis as "the process of gradual or unconscious assimilation of ideas, knowledge, etc." Gradual is defined as "taking place or progressing slowly or by degrees." Assimilation is defined as "the process of taking in and fully understanding information or ideas."

God is doing nothing without you being sober through gradual increases and bursts of his presence and progression by what we say yes to, and the fully conscious assimilation, or taking in a deeper understanding of him working through us as individuals, as this is a relationship, and it takes two. Now once the root of Jesus is realized really good, then there becomes moments where he allows the seeds he planted along the way to be released as growth spurts that you did not even know were deep down inside of you, which ends up being your assigned ministries.

We must get to know God for ourselves for the Holy Spirit will lead you into all things classified, the things, that will not ever be presented through a textbook, Zoom call, or sermon, for God is the WORD, and only the WORD will withstand the times, and restore our lost times.

For it is God alone that gives man promotions, confirmed in 1 Corinthians 3:6-8AMP, which clearly explains that it does take two; it is according to what we put in it. And God says,

I planted, Apollos watered, but God [all the while] was causing the growth. So, neither is the one who plants nor the one who waters anything, but [only] God who causes the growth. He who plants, and he who waters are one [in importance and esteem, working toward the same purpose]; but each will receive his own reward according to his own labor.

It is only God who can distribute favor between Him and Man. According to Luke 2:52, when we are about our Father's business, God says, *"And Jesus increased in wisdom and stature, and in favor with God and men."*

Truth is my start of legacy is when I put God first. A legacy is that transmitted by or received from an ancestor, or predecessor, or from the past. A legacy is something that is meant to outlive or outlast you. Deep calls upon deep are the results of building a true legacy, where your fruit shall remain.

Before I put in the work, my unpacked truth defined legacy as an insurance policy, that would take care of the deceased's funeral, their debt, and a few good years of good life coupled with unstable emotions, worldly attitudes, broken spirits, and unpaid cycles of spiritual debt. That is what I thought legacy meant, life insurance, and all the characteristics of the deceased individuals who are no longer with us. Even the people that I knew of whose businesses, as a child, still thrived off the world's production, and acquired temporary things that could be replaced, but never secured the method to creating generational wealth. Now my understanding of Generational wealth is that it still will generate multiple residuals, increased paths of resources, covenant partnerships, and recurring subscriptions, even when we or our seeds, retire or leave this earth.

As I became more mature in the things of God, he began to introduce to me what legacy means and that I would be the first in my family to live and build a life of legacy. Part of my legacy is verified in the word, to help be a witness to others and to encourage them to teach what they have learned through the Holy Ghost, speaking to me that they will desire to build their own legacies with no point of references.

II Timothy 2:2 NIV confirms how the concept of legacy is transferred by faith to others, *"And the things you have heard me say in the presence of many witnesses entrusted to reliable people who will also be qualified to teach others."*

Generational poverty, in my revelation, is not just about money. It is about the lack of developing our spiritual wealth, which is the fruit of the spirit, found in Galatians 5: 22-23 NIV, saying, *"But the fruit of the Spirit is love, joy, peace, forbearance, kindness, goodness, faithfulness, gentleness and self-control. Against such things, there is no law."*

I was not left a legacy from my biological mom nor my biological father, God rest their souls. I believe that not receiving a legacy, honestly, created a push in me by God to do the work, to build my character in God, so that I could be the first to break the cycle of generational deficiencies and atrocities, the carryover of curses, the poverty of bad spirits, the poverty of bad attitudes, the poverty of underprivileged mindsets, the poverty of self-sabotage, and the poverty of comparison, to name a few.

Generational poverty through my research is caused by self-reinforcing mechanisms. Self-reinforcing is defined as a process whereby individuals control their own behavior by rewarding themselves when a certain standard of performance has been attained or surpassed. In other words, read it again, where individuals control their own behavior, allowing flesh to rule.

Self-infliction is defined as the infliction of pain or suffering on oneself. Self-infliction can be covered up in other actions such as playing the victim, the exaggeration of victimhood, the blaming or diversion of true accountability, in a subconscious attempt that think through osmosis, we get to our place of generational legacy, but the truth is, we all have knowing or unknowingly, played the victim, blamed someone else for our lack of understanding, as a child, as an adult, and even some elderly people still have not fully grasped this concept.

We will not get to our place in legacy without putting in the work. We may have submitted to this role to scathe directions, of the steps it takes, for the real work. The work that must be put in, to get back the motivational thrusts. We need to demonstrate a level of dedication, to become our best selves, to grow at a more consistent rate, and maintain a healthier mindset of seeing ourselves in better space and place.

The key of Self-reinforcement is Self-infliction. This is our pathway of denying truth and could nurture our outright unbelief and disagreement with God. As a result, this cycle of self-infliction will persist until there is some type of outside prevention. The protection and the outside prevention is the Holy Ghost. The Holy Ghost/The Holy Spirit is our Divine Mediator and Protector, which secures our path to Divine Recognizance that restoration is very much needed.

God has put in motion for me to build a legacy for my children. This means that I will be able to leave them with a heritage, more than material possessions, intellectual rights, residual income, land, and more in Jesus' Name, Amen. I have hope and faith that I will be able to leave them things that they cannot quantify or count with their natural eyes, that my children's children and great-grandchildren to the 10th generation and beyond, and that they will be superbly blessed as a result of my level of obedience to God's call on my natural life.

INTRODUCTION

This is the preboarding announcement for Flight 3333 to A Three-Dimensional Legacy. Please have your boarding pass and identification ready.

Welcome to Flight 3333. You are now boarding. I am Vanessa S. Brown your flight attendant, who will be assisting you throughout this flight. As you board, remember that all luggage must be secure and have been processed prior to boarding this flight. Please fasten your belt of truth. We ask that your breastplate of righteousness be in an upright position for takeoff. Please turn off all prior knowledge and put on your helmet of salvation. All distractions that cause adverse effects are prohibited for the duration of the flight. Thank you for choosing Kingdom Airlines. Enjoy your flight.

We are now preparing for takeoff. We may need to board connecting flights in order to complete this journey. This flight has a sectioned manual that provides the details of this entire journey.

Our first section is called "Reserved and Weighty". Our connecting sections are called "Divine Attitude", "Divine Assembly", and "Divine Acceleration"

The date is August 10, 2023. We are experiencing clear skies and sunny weather, with a high of 88 degrees this morning. We are approximately seventeen minutes ahead of schedule.

As God coined this move, I am to ensure the facilitation of this flight remains smooth, but the winds (Holy Spirit) may move, as he will, on the pages of your hearts as I pour out what God has developed in me.

We have been called into training with Abba with strategic steps and outlines as we travel. So let us ensure we have our full spiritual armor on, and we continue matriculating past our registration into our officiation. An officiant is defined as what makes our kingdom's adoption legal.

My prayer is that you are able to chew on, process, and put these instructions into action. What is in this book will help solidify your identity in Christ and confirm your rank in the kingdom of God. So, ensure your belt of truth is securely fastened with the helmet of salvation and the breastplate of righteousness as we lay the foundation with the mind that we serve God.

Section 1

RESERVED AND WEIGHTY

Quote - " Even in reserve, you still got to serve. "Though reserved, your silence speaks volumes, and with every measured word, you carry the weight of wisdom and depth. In a world that often rushes to speak, your thoughtful restraint is a beacon of strength and profound influence. Quiet strength lies in the hearts of the reserved; their words may be few, but each one carries the weight of wisdom and the power to inspire profound change."

A FLIGHT TO A THREE-DIMENSIONAL LEGACY

The experience was truly extraordinary—ascending to a place I've never been, higher than I've ever been. Here, I am carrying the things of God with grace, structure, and order. Then, a profound shift occurred. Things seemed to be spiraling down. I found myself in a new place, back on reserve, and now in a state of waiting. This weighty reserve compels me to leave my baggage in the past.

Before we dive into the reserved and weighty section, it is important we provide some clarity on this section and how being reserved and weighty led me to submit to assigned authorities on a greater level. It also helped me to acquire the will to maintain a divine attitude when my flesh did not want to comply. It is vital that process and order are a part of this manuscript, not my process and my order, but God's divine process and order, which brings reassurance and security. During my reserved and weighty life, I learned the true meaning of God working a far weightier Glory that shall be revealed. Well, Let's GO!!!!

The word 'reserve ', as defined by Oxford languages, means to refrain from being used or retained for future use. From a biblical perspective, it signifies something set aside or preserved for a specific purpose or time. This concept is echoed in the scripture, 'There is a season, a time appointed for everything and a time for every delight and event or purpose under heaven' – Ecclesiastes 3:1AMP. God often reserves certain blessings, judgments, or remnant groups for His divine purposes. This is His way of safeguarding what He deems precious or necessary for the future fulfillment of His plans. Another layer to the biblical meaning of reserve involves the notion of restraint or holding back. In this case, God is encouraging us to exercise self-control and patience. This is evident in the scripture Proverbs 16:32, which tells us to be slow to anger, suggesting that reserving one's wrath is a sign of strength and wisdom. This aspect of reserve underscores the importance of measured behavior and the spiritual discipline to withhold immediate impulses in favor of a more considered, righteous response. In essence, the biblical meaning of reserve encompasses ideas of preservation, restraint, and divine assurance, all of which underline God's meticulous planning and the importance of faith and patience in the spiritual journey, bringing comfort and peace.

On the other hand, Oxford languages define **weighty** as heavy, of great seriousness, and of greater importance. The term "weighty" carries significant connotations beyond its literal sense of physical heaviness in the Bible. It often denotes a sense of importance, gravitas, or profound impact. For instance, in the Old Testament, the Hebrew word "kavod" is frequently translated as "glory" but can also mean "weight" or "heaviness." This term describes God's glory, indicating a substantial, authoritative, and majestic presence. When something is described as weighty in a biblical context, it implies that it holds considerable significance and demands respect and contemplation. In the New Testament, the Apostle Paul uses the concept of weightiness in his letters. In 2 Corinthians 4:17, he contrasts the "light momentary affliction" with an "eternal weight of glory beyond all comparison." Here, Paul emphasizes that the present's trials and sufferings are insignificant compared to the profound and everlasting glory that awaits believers. This comparison highlights the enduring and substantial nature of God's promises and the ultimate reward for faithfulness. Thus, in the biblical sense, "weighty" encompasses the ideas of significance, authority, and lasting impact.

The word weighty while writing this book was revealed to me as one who is pregnant with God's Will and plan. Weighty can also mean a higher level of emotional intelligence. The oil that has been reserved is being squeezed out of a person, which will carry others further into their own gifts and callings.

Reserved and Training

Whewwww, in my mind, I was already struggling with my feelings, which was the wrong focus. I have been up since 06:00, traveling, and it is now 18:00, and it is getting dark. However, by faith, I made it. I am physically hungry and wondering if I made the right steps, but little did I remember, GOD DID IT. My full-circle dream is really materializing, and the LORD has ordered my steps.

I stood with bated breath (anticipation) while waiting for the shuttle bus to pick us up. All I could imagine was I was going to the middle of nowhere. Where are you, Vanessa? I did not fully understand it, but I had just entered the next era of my life. I accepted my CJO (conditional job offer) with the airlines a few weeks ago, and my whole world just shifted. My entire world has not just moved but shifted up. A conditional offer means it is not finished, meaning that until I complete all the steps, the necessary requirements to receive the job offer fully are still looked at as a condition. It reminds me of the scripture, *"Study and do your best to present yourself to God approved, a workman tested by trial who has no reason to be ashamed, accurately handling and skillfully teaching the word of truth"* – 2 Timothy 2:15AMP.

We arrived at the training facility at night. When I stepped off the shuttle, I felt like I had walked several miles, and now I am out of breath. It looked like it had been snowing all day; it was icy, and the temperature was in the teens. Brrrrrrrr. This is the first day of my reservation. I walked into a different dimension. This is huge. I did not know what to expect, nor what I would have to adjust to. There was a sense that I was about to experience things in a way that I could have never imagined. Why? Because when God says he will do a new thing, can we not perceive it? Only God can do these things.

We were all pre-assigned roommates for training. When we arrive at the training facility tonight, we will meet for the first time. We had to welcome ourselves and others. I went by the front desk and retrieved my roommate's name and my key to our lodge. As I proceeded to walk to my assigned lodge, I began to get nervous, thinking about what would happen if my roommate did not like me. What if my roommate requested someone else but was denied? I was thinking like I hope that we have some similarities and that we have something in common, not just material things, but that we both have similar or like beliefs to reduce excess stress while training for the next few weeks. I walked into my room and met my roommate. When we saw each other, it was like she had been going through similar internal thoughts, and we both shared our prayers. We both said God knows best. We made a vow that we would both make it through by prayer and encouragement of each other, while respecting each other's differences. Yes, we experienced a few moments where the enemy tried to disrupt the unity, but we would respect each other and talked with God in prayer. I reminded my roommate that the enemy would love for us to give up and throw up our hands. However, God stepped into our space by our invitation, and He worked it out for the both of us. We knew from day one when we met, that we had come too far, and that we had been through too much to turn back or to shrink back. Thank God for divine partnerships along the road to destiny.

I reminded myself that I must be patient with this new life, this reserved life, this weighty life. Not only has my environment changed, but the altitude of my life has shifted up as well. The air is thin, and I had to learn how to breathe in a new elevation, a weightier level, called the reserve life.

Throughout my airline training, I felt like I was back in college. I started reminiscing about my college life. There is so much new information, and different procedures were being introduced. It was like being born again and learning to walk again in the aviation world. It is the reprogramming of what I viewed as a normal life. Our in-flight recruiters and staff, and instructors would forewarn us of little caveats we may face while on reserve. They warned us of what not to try and what not to do. This was so that we had a fair view of what was happening to avoid misinterpretations. In other words, it may not be exactly a walk in the park. They would encourage us that if we could just walk out our first year of being a flight attendant, what is waiting on the other side would be well worth it.

Going into this new life, I was determined to make it through training, and I extrapolated (made up in my mind) to walk through the first year of being a flight attendant with mercy and grace for myself. The reserved life of a flight attendant leans toward a much weightier lifestyle, a lifestyle that I had to learn to suffer and smile while getting better, not bitter. Being on reserve made me understand I was being set up to finish the race. Fast forward, I passed all the written and final exams with A's. Once I passed my written tests, it was time for my IOE (Initial Operating Experience). God blessed me, and I was able to pass my IOE. Now, I had to learn to walk in greatness consistently each time I was called off the bench to work.

As we wait on reserve, we begin to evolve mentally, spiritually, physically, emotionally, psychologically, and physiologically. This is especially true when we get to the part where we cross over from milk to meat. We go through a threshing floor process like God separating the wheat from the tare. We individually are being drained of the past naysayers, past poison, that once dirtied our blood. Just like when one must be hooked up to an IV, grace and mercy are pumped into our spirit, even our marrow. Dictionary.com defines marrow as the inmost or essential part, while insecurity and unbelief are pumped out of our spirit.

We can't change fly coordinates as the Holy Spirit (Captain GOD) will always beat the hidden plots, plans, and agendas of managers, customers, employees, and crew. Thank God the captain can override misconfigured coordinates. Now, let us look a little deeper into the Critical Phases of Flight while being on reserve.

A FLIGHT TO A THREE-DIMENSIONAL LEGACY

Critical Phases of Flight

"Please ensure your seats are in the upright position, tray tables are stowed, window shades are up, laptops are stored in the overhead bins, and electronic devices are set to flight mode as we take off (or land)."

While on reserve, you must follow the safety demo process, learning how to put on a mask yourself first before attempting to save someone else. For each departure from an old place, there is an arrival in a new place, and there is a critical phase of flight associated with it. During the critical phase of flight, it is important to recall what steps you have taken to demonstrate safety, secure the flight deck, and communicate with the crew and the customers on a flight. This is also a great time to remember how to handle the unknown, surprise attacks, and/or an emergency landing (for both water and land). Some of the general phases of flights include the planning phase, takeoff phase, climb phase, cruise phase, descent phase, approach phase, and taxi phase.

In the planning phase, in flying, and in real life, it is important to gather all the necessary tools and skills to carry out the promise throughout the flight phases so that when you take off, you will not be surprised by what may occur during the climbing phase. Planning is a crucial aspect of life, and many scriptures emphasize the importance of foresight and preparation. One such verse is Proverbs 16:3, which states, *"Commit to the Lord whatever you do, and he will establish your plans."* This verse underscores the importance of aligning one's plans with divine guidance and seeking spiritual approval in the planning process. It reassures that when plans are committed to a higher purpose, they are more likely to succeed. Another significant scripture is found in Jeremiah 29:11, which reads, *"For I know the plans I have for you," declares the Lord, "plans to prosper you and not to harm you, plans to give you hope and a future."* This verse reflects the belief that there is a divine plan for each individual, filled with hope and prosperity. It encourages people to trust in a higher power's wisdom and benevolence, even when their own plans seem uncertain or challenging.

Lastly, Proverbs 21:5 offers practical wisdom: *"The plans of the diligent lead to profit as surely as haste leads to poverty."* This verse highlights the value of diligent and thoughtful planning. It warns against the pitfalls of rushing into decisions without careful consideration. Together, these verses from the Bible provide a balanced perspective on the importance of planning, emphasizing the need for divine guidance, trust in a higher purpose, and the virtues of diligence and careful preparation.

As we reach the cruise phase, this is the place to clean out any weights that can affect the next transition, clean out anything familiar that would have us handle the next season like we handled the last season. Further, we have already leaped over bounds reaching the altitude that we should be functioning on for this season in our life. So, when we reach the cruise phase, or I call it the rest phase, it is important to rest during the cruise altitudes because in due time we will be ready to descend out of one phase into the next phase of flight.

When presented with reserved and weighty situations, we learn skills to abase and abound from other senior flight attendants, pilots, first officers, and most importantly, our FAM (flight attendant manual). With each flight experience, we learn how to prepare differently and how to wait differently. *"But those who wait for the Lord who expect, look for, and hope in Him Will gain new strength and renew their power; They will lift up their wings and rise up close to God like eagles rising toward the sun; They will run and not become weary, They will walk and not grow tired"* – Isaiah 40:31AMP. We also learn more effective ways of dropping excess waste and leaving all carry-on belongings in case of an emergency evacuation. *"Casting all your cares, all your anxieties, all your worries, and all your concerns, once and for all on Him, for He cares about you with deepest affection and watches over you very carefully"* – 1 Peter 5:7AMP. We intentionally develop amicable ways to preserve our fuel and energy and increase our peace. Our peace increases when we keep our minds focused on God.

During the critical phase of flights, we learn how to love our enemies with a joyful attitude. The most critical point that I learned while being on reserve as a flight attendant is that God is omniscient and His knowledge, the word, is timeless. I believe this is the most critical point because of the many levels of uncertainties each day one walks into a more reserved and weightier lifestyle. During critical phases of flight, it is crucial that we are laser-focused so we can be more concise in our communication, procedures, and actions and respond appropriately to situations. Whether you are on reserve for an airline, ministry, or marketplace, Psalm 55:22 encourages us and tells us what to do with our cares: *"Cast your cares on the Lord, and He will sustain you; He will never let the righteous be shaken."*

Devalued Reserves

This section includes a reminder that we must value ourselves just as much as we expect others to. It is an upfront reminder: "Remember You Are Worthy."

There were instances, even in my life on reserves, where I was treated as if I was easily replaced even though I knew in my heart I wasn't. I had to encounter the thought that tried to present itself to me. So, at the beginning of my adulthood, I would let it bother me, but no more. If you are reading this book, you should know that you aren't easily replaced either. There are things inside of you that only you can do how you would, so never take devaluations to heart. Most times, they distract us from the greater that is within us! That's a fact!

We will face situations in life that make us question who we are and where we are, but we must remain calm, trusting God through each process. Pay attention to God, not our emotions, not what society says, not what the media says. We must keep a YES unto the LORD as God is elevating us. We may work a job that does not consider the time we put in or the ways God has made on our behalf; however, this does not mean we stop considering our value. This is a great time to list our values and the good in us before we start to get sidetracked.

We hear a lot about not paying attention to others who don't know your value. But do you know your worth? Truth be told, you devalue, and people devalue what they don't know, understand, or cannot control. This is why it is urgent that you know who you are. Whether you're having a great or challenging day, don't lose sight of your exponential worth! I can't count how many times I've encouraged others and shouted in the atmosphere that I believe in another person, but I can count on my fingers and toes how many times I've shouted this to myself. Don't get me wrong, as a coach, I'm always in the undergird position to encourage myself, but saying I believe in you, Vanessa, comes far and few between. So, let's start today by speaking it over ourselves: I believe in you, Vanessa (insert your name).

My attitude is Yes; I will trust you, LORD, while I wait on reserve. Yes, I will trust that you have already set aside a seat for me in my new place. Yes, because you are preparing me to be a flight attendant naturally for the marketplace and spiritually for your kingdom. Lord, I do not long to rush you.

When you are on reserves, whether in the marketplace or ministry, you and I go through a point of valuation, as do those who decide to put you on reserves. Sometimes situations make you second guess your value, but don't do it. Like the scripture says in Proverbs 3:5-6 NIV, *"Trust in the Lord with all your heart and lean not on your own understanding; in all your ways submit to him, and he will make your paths straight."*

Brace, Brace, Brace, just because you are in a waiting period, don't negate your skills or your value; remember the good in you. See, we must maintain our faith and hope; our faith is our currency. We cannot allow someone to diminish our value and our currency, regardless of the environment we encounter on the road to transition from being on reserve to being used. You see, it is at an appointed time that we begin to be used mightily, that we gain momentum and stability, and the wisdom and understanding we need to walk into the next season, our next assignment. We all have assignments that must be completed.

In life, we go through periods where God has promised us something, but as we walk through the process, we forget that we have assigned seats. We forget that our seat is not based on our physical location but on our spiritual assignments. Our seat is based on our heart posture, not our conditions. There are assignments associated with our position in God. It is critical that we communicate and spend time in worship with God even more during devalued periods of our lives and that we do not seek the approval of others. It is God who makes our name great. By attempting to gain acceptance through man, we miss our opportunity to be one-on-one with God, who is our creator and our blueprint. For God approved David, and he has already approved us.

While waiting, it can become weighty because of what you have experienced or experiencing. The experience can seem catastrophic and unyielding, but by faith, let's remain steady in the storm and be ready to crossover. *"Having been deeply rooted in Him and now being built up in Him and becoming increasingly more established in your faith, just as you were taught, and overflowing in it with gratitude"* – Colossians 2:7 AMP.

When it doesn't look like there's a seat for us, we must intentionally trust God. Even when there's unexpected turbulence and disorder in this world, we can trust that God is still in control. When the winds are choppy and things don't go as planned, we can trust God. He makes the difference in time that was lost. He irons out the clad opposition and multiple obstacles with one word.

Reserved and Waiting

In the bible, the concept of "wait" carries profound spiritual significance, encompassing themes of patience, trust, and hope. Biblically, waiting is often associated with a period of anticipation when one trusts God's timing and plan. It also involves a sense of surrender and reliance on divine wisdom rather than human understanding. Wait encompasses an active, trusting, and hopeful posture toward God's sovereignty and timing.

The reserved process is necessary as it allows one to be refueled, restored, refined, renewed, and equipped with new tools for the next place. It is a time to be built up for something even greater. It is not a one-time process; it's a continuous process as one continuously elevates in the kingdom. When you're reserved and waiting, it's good to have a crew, a network, that has your back, especially during these difficult and weighty transitions. A crew that knows how to handle tough times and problems gracefully. *"For where two or three are gathered in My name meeting together as My followers, I am there among them."* – Matthew 18:20 AMP. When we are reserved and waiting, we must always be ready to move, ready to shift, ready to flow, and ready to be used when God makes it happen. Be ready with a smile and leap into good faith in your spirit. He knows the route we must take. Job 23:10 reminds us that God is not slight on his promises, and he knows what is happening to us, and has examined us, and we will pass with honors. There could be many reasons we are put on reserve. An example is when we have not finished what God has already assigned us to do. So, we must walk by faith and not by sight to complete the works given. Faith without works is dead. So, take the necessary steps towards what God has revealed and given you to do. Through obedience to God, we can be divinely elevated, unhindered, and unchecked. Now that our attitude has begun to be revamped and our mindset has been polished, we can go forward with a divine attitude.

A FLIGHT TO A THREE-DIMENSIONAL LEGACY

Reserved and Weighty Discussion

From frustration to fruit from insensitivity to sensitivity; from anger and sadness to emotional, physical, spiritual, and mental stability. From warfare to wellness; from sadness to joy; from messiness to meekness; from nosey to nobility come on; from fruit to more fruit to much fruit we all must go through our personal walk through the tabernacle to successfully fulfill the assignments from GOD.

1. What are a few steps you can now take in confidence, knowing that you are reserved for purpose and on purpose?

_____

_____

_____

_____

_____

_____

_____

2. How will you view yourself going forward?

_____

_____

_____

_____

_____

_____

_____

3. How do you view challenges now that you have read this section?

_____

_____

_____

_____

_____

_____

_____

Section 2

THE DIVINE ATTITUDE

Quote - " A divine attitude encompasses clear thinking, well wishes, and the desire to increase the quality of life and the life of those around us; this is a divine attitude."

A FLIGHT TO A THREE-DIMENSIONAL LEGACY

Step aboard 'A Flight to A Three-Dimensional Legacy' with me, your personal flight attendant, Vanessa Brown. This extraordinary journey, Flight 3333, is a one-of-a-kind experience divided into three distinct Sections, each with its own set of mini-segments and private flight segments. Every section concludes with thought-provoking transitional questions, guiding you from one spiritual altitude to the next. This carefully structured approach ensures you derive the maximum benefit from this transformative reading experience. As you embark on this literary flight, I invite you to review the overview and disclosures.

Overview and Disclosure of A Flight to A Three-Dimensional Legacy

The 'armor of God' serves as the cornerstone of this book, its pieces gradually revealing themselves as you delve deeper into the text and even long after you've finished reading. It is God's will for you to prosper as your soul prospers. In this context, 'prospering' means personal growth, achievement, thriving, and flourishing. It entails enhancing your personal integrity, moral courage, and nurturing a righteous heart. To achieve this, we must renounce our worldly ways, reshape our beliefs, and gain a deeper understanding of God's principles.

There may be some embryonic falsehoods of a divine attitude along the way. I urge you to rebuild your attitude to reach new altitudes of hope and impart potent faith. I understand that some of you requested a change in seating and position upon boarding the aircraft, and some requested to be around people who know you and do not challenge you. We will review the load balances before departure to determine the necessary adjustments.

In the reading, you will receive instructions on how your attitude can be maintained by the time invested in reading the word of God, which is how to command your day so you will be prepared to divide the whole counsel of the word rightly. Study and do your best to present yourself as God-approved, ensuring an understanding of your intake of His Word. Most importantly, you will learn how to respond with great courage to overcome and/or understand the "The Baffled Transfer of Stewardship," 'a concept that challenges us to take responsibility for our spiritual growth and development. This is a call to action, a challenge to rise above and embrace the divine courage within you.

Rest assured, we are now addressing any load imbalances in the cabin. I personally want to express my gratitude for choosing to fly with Kingdom Airlines on Flight 3333. Your safety is our top priority.

Fix the Load Imbalances

Attitude determines altitude, so how can we truly go up and maintain up if our altitude is not in full alignment with God's plan and will for our lives? Maintaining up is not cheating up. It's walking in truth while being blessed! It's not having the attitude of calling attention to oneself but allowing God to be God. We must remind ourselves that we have help! *"For the Lord GOD will help Me; Therefore, I will not be disgraced; Therefore, I have set My face like a flint, And I know that I will not be ashamed."* (Isaiah 50:7)

We are aboard flights that may have to be canceled or rebooked due to human errors, so the load becomes imbalanced. This results in people's seats scattered all over the plane, with more seats in one cabin than another. It triggers a load imbalance, so some things must be shifted to ensure the safety and security of our flight.

It is just like when we are working on a situation, and it seems everything is all over the place. If we are not careful, we can find ourselves trying to fix what is not meant to be fixed. We can find ourselves trying to combine the things that have already expired with those that have yet to begin. I had a friend that took a trip to Chicago. She had a carry-on bag that could be adjusted in size if packed right. It seems nice, right? Well, she boarded the plane and had to put her bag in the console. Her luggage was bigger than the console. She had to decrease the size to try and get it to fit. Even after reducing the size, her bag still wouldn't fit. What do you believe could have been the problem in this scenario? We often mix and overload our luggage with what is old and new. We try to make old things, habits, and mindsets work in new places and then become frustrated when it doesn't work. The Bible says, "Old things have passed, behold all things have become new," meaning that we have to declutter the old, forgetting those things that are behind us, and press toward the mark for the prize of the high calling of God in Christ Jesus. What's the solution? Everything comes with an expiration date. Some expiration dates can be renewed, but that's another topic for another time. We must not mix old (expired) wine with new wineskins. Let go of the things that have expired in your life. It's called decluttering. To declutter means to remove mess or clutter from a place. It is to organize and prioritize one's commitments. Her luggage would not fit in the console because it needed to be decluttered and not reduced in size. We can find ourselves fighting the pruning/decluttering process, preferring to lower our standards, carrying an overload of clutter, feeling weighed down and heavy, and unable to function fully and operate as God has called us to operate.

Clutter limits our ability to fully develop values and actions that promote our true purpose in life. When there is clutter, whether in our mind or heart, it causes us to lack peace, contentment, and forgiveness. Take a moment and look at what is in your luggage. What do you need to declutter? What do you need to let go of? What do you need to release? If you are unsure, ask God to reveal it to you and strengthen you through the process of decluttering/pruning. When going through pruning, you are releasing total control, letting God have his way. *"He cuts off every branch in me that bears no fruit, while every branch that does bear fruit he prunes so that it will be even more fruitful."* -John 15:2-3 NIV.

"Boarding is complete. The main cabin door has been closed. Flight attendants prepare the doors for departure and stand by for all calls. Hello, this is Vanessa. All doors are verified, and the cabin is secure." Our flight time may vary based on our ability to flow and accept our calls in real time.

Divine Attitude is accepting and cutting ties with losses and regrets. We cannot make other people see our worth on each level. Let them walk away. We are not the problem. It is true that our mental inconsistencies may or may not be regulated, so if our attitude and mind are not upright when knowledge enters, it causes more baffled transfers of stewardship. These inconsistencies can often have us release our rights to the gift of our measure of faith if we are not receptive. If we are not teachable, we miss the opportunity to be taught to rightly divide the whole counsel of the Word of God. Being teachable will speak to what is available in us and what treasures God has planted inside us without asking for it. It comes with the measure of faith each of us has been given. (see Romans 12:3 KJV)

Some people have never been introduced to the fact that this is what baffled transfers of stewardship look like. It can truly go either way, depending on who is responsible for us or which options we choose (our will) when we come of age. With obedience, we are introduced to uncompromising leaders and teachers of the Faith who will help us the rest of the way. We either choose earthly wisdom or heavenly wisdom. In simpler terms, we can choose our Flesh to orchestrate and alleviate or the Holy Spirit to dominate and demonstrate. I once denied this truth, but it is so, and so it is, and it is true anyhow. This is true, especially regarding how our minds can bend the way our voices speak. We can speak the truth about ourselves or believe the lies we have been told.

Let's discuss a few examples. You have a little girl who has been raised hearing that she is a princess, beautiful, smart, intelligent, kind, loved, liked, cherished, protected, safe, brilliant, pretty, and gorgeous, just like someone who may have been raised and spoken to as a little boy, that he is a provider, a protector, a prince, handsome, cute, loving, strong, witty, charming, sweet, and a warrior. Later in life, these humble foundations crumble in the unforeseen years of denied self-worth, wrong community, wrong perceptions of others, domestic violence, and verbal, mental, and financial abuse. Everybody's tolerance varies, so for a stronger person, it may take ten years to fold, but for a person who does not have these humble foundations, it takes two years to break the preset wall of faith. So, the people affected take a 180-degree turn due to being a recipient of the lies demonstrated before them, opposite of these humble foundational words imparted to them. Yes, words have POWER. Now, this result can worsen if this little girl or little boy gets out of one abusive relationship and shortly enters another one. Then, the wall of faith is blurred, blemished, and not traceable, and the individual is lost. I am a witness.

This is also true when a girl/boy/man/woman is treated one way at home and another way in education, church, or ministry affiliations, which results in extra baggage, extra warfare, extra bondage, and an extra layer of onions. That is just our mind extrapolating outwards.

In this context, what a person has experienced may look like the conclusion of the matter, the wrapping up of the thesis of their life, based on the statistics, when only a portion of our inherent beliefs have been marred by the wrong perspectives and the inconsistent ability to function in emotionally healthy partnerships and relationships.

The word says, *"A double-minded man is unstable in all his ways"*- James 1:8. Our attitudes will be tested as we mature and reclaimed to our elections. Our absolute will be tested. Our election will come into the fire. But be steadfast, immovable, always abounding in grace when this happens.

When we enter our acceleration season, remember we will be tested in our honor and integrity. From my experience, unclean spirits seem to find a way to make us second-guess ourselves and the value of who we are. This is why we must consider emotionally detoxing our minds and hearts regularly and consistently. We must slay every emotional giant!

A FLIGHT TO A THREE-DIMENSIONAL LEGACY

Maintaining a Divine Attitude

"My attitude is my gratitude. Not that I speak from any personal need, for I have learned to be content and self-sufficient through Christ, satisfied to the point where I am not disturbed or uneasy regardless of my circumstances." — Philippians 4:11 AMP

Our attitude should not be whether we are qualified to do something but whether we have the heart to lead the mission as God has directed and revealed to us. Will we have the integrity to uphold our end of the deal? Having a divine attitude bears a message, and the messenger (Jesus) is the message. We are creating space to expand and express ourselves daily, having the desire to stay consistent in thoughts and prayers unto God.

Here are a few ways to create space to expand your mindset:

1. Demonstrating love for yourself and others creates safe spaces for others to sit, share, and support. (Luke 10:27)

2. By maturely expressing yourself, consider others before yourself sometimes. (Philippians 2:3-4)

3. By speaking up for people who may not know how to speak up for themselves. (Proverbs 31:8-9)

4. By not alluding to or hinting about things, we learn to speak the truth so that more people are made free. (Ephesians 4:15, John 8:31-32)

5. By believing, God will make all things better concerning us and lead us to greater heights and greater opportunities. (Romans 8:28)

6. By standing together with like-minded leaders and people who want more for themselves and their families. (Romans 15:5-6, Philippians 2:2-8)

7. By learning how to communicate clearly and peacefully, noticing that there's an actual two-way conversation occurring. (Ephesians 4:29)

By the end of this section, you will have identified other ways to express a divine attitude and embrace the call with a clear mindset.

Check Air Filters, Trash, and Lavatories

As we continue the segment of the flight, let us solidify our attitudes, check our filters, and check our EFAP (enhanced forward attendant panel). These things may be generational barriers, family triggers, addictions, mindset, pride, emotional instability, failed relationships and marriages, and so much more.

I am a person who tries not to complain at all or very little. During the process, I accepted jobs beneath my spiritual pay grade, trying to pay worldly expenses and overhead costs. Let me give you an example. I took jobs where I could not be myself. I had to minimize who I was to allow others to feel better about themselves or the people they were connected to. My discernment would shine through and allow me to see through the individuals that came to break my spirit. As a result, I ended up feeling mentally stagnated, dwarfed, distant, and debunked in my spirit, not understanding why I had to experience moments like this. *"Do not conform to the pattern of this world but be transformed by the renewing of your mind. Then you will be able to test and approve what God's will is – his good, pleasing, and perfect will"* – Romans 12:2 NIV.

You notice I said I felt. The key is to leave our emotions on the sidelines, starving for attention, and the enemy that came for you will flee. You see, we can't be going around feeling sorry for ourselves due to other people's disembodied attitudes we are met with. We must remain focused on that which remains and flexible enough to line up with God's assignments and plans, not our own, not our best friends (or best friend's) suggestions. This is between you and God. We don't know what demons people are fighting off. *"For we wrestle not against flesh and blood, but against principalities, against powers, against the rulers of the darkness of this world, against spiritual wickedness in high places"* – Ephesians 6:12 KJV. So, instead of interrupting our peace, pray and give it to God until he heals every part of us, thus making us mature and whole.

As God matured me in my spirit, I demonstrated the fruit of the spirit, such as temperance. In challenging situations, it is best to increase grace and mercy for those assigned to try to deter us. This is why we must surround ourselves with people who want to see us thrive, not survive, win, and not lose; those who love, support, and understand where we are going.

I am not specifically referring to financial support. Truth be told, mental and emotional support can cover us better than any amount of money provided, for it is how we perceive a thing. If our attitude is up and we are optimistic and ready to go, we can make the best out of whatever resources are available because our attitude is bright, clear, and teachable. In addition, other resources become accessible to us.

We must rest regularly, as debris can come and clog our daily filters, thinking, and hearing. Let us throw away all our old C-folds, dirty filters, and garbage, such as toxic situations and old, smelly situations, that sometimes reside in our inner lavatories. Most of the time, no one knows about these areas except us and God. May we remove those things from our house of memories and learn what should remain and what needs to be evacuated by command immediately.

I pray that we become lovers of structure and order so that we may continue to ascend higher. Remember your why, and do not let anyone move your WHY needle. This is what keeps us solid, tried, and grounded. We must focus through all chaos as victory is on the other side. We struggle to fit where we don't belong. We need only ourselves to fit through the eye of destiny. Let us walk in divine protection on this uncommon journey to a destiny with no weight (baggage).

A FLIGHT TO A THREE-DIMENSIONAL LEGACY

Are You Ready for an Uncommon Journey?

What is your uncommon journey? God adjusted the bit on whatever it is, so you overcame or will overcome it.

Our attitudes are somewhat shaped early on by our experiences. Then, as we mature, our attitudes are shaped by scriptural wisdom and truth as we grow up, as we journey from faith to faith and glory to glory. You may ask what an uncommon journey is. It is the road that's less traveled. It could be not being able to consider our knowledge so that we may be able to handle the journey. It could be a journey of being misunderstood or overlooked. It could mean that you were handled more strictly by peers and family as opposed to the next sibling or best friend. It could also mean you had to endure more pain or pressure in a short amount of time as opposed to someone who may not have experienced excess trauma or frequent life changes and adaptation. Yes, we may be walking in what seems like the shadow of death, but keep moving forward, as *"the race is not given to the swift nor the strong, but to the one who endures until the end"* – Ecclesiastes 9:11. This is major in developing a divine attitude.

Being a flight attendant made me understand what being fearless means and helped me embrace trusting God to keep me. While in flight attendant training, there wasn't a day that I didn't fear the unknown. Since I knew nothing about aviation, nothing was familiar or common. Each day, I was embracing an uncommon journey. Sure, I've flown before, but it was nothing like being trained to work on flights. It was like a cross between a chaperone mixed with good customer service, a hostess mixed with good logistics knowledge, or a Fireman or RN without the state licensing process. We were told in training to flow, like liquid, with positivity as we sway backward and forward. Either way, no day has been the same. We can have great days, and then up pops a lousy day. One might say the rollercoaster depends on the crew to which you are assigned, but in essence, it depends on the attitude that you carry. Your surroundings shouldn't change or depict your attitude. It is the light of your attitude that changes and depicts your surroundings. Make it a great day, no matter what it may look like. Count it all joy.

Being a flight attendant reminded me that just like we have no control over the family we have been assigned, it is the same when we are assigned bases and different flight crews. However, as flight attendants, we can pick a person to be our buddy. Buddies are like our extended families. It can be the same challenges faced in our personal lives and professions outside aviation. We never know what we may be placed in or where we may be asked to serve.

Being a flight attendant has not been easy, but it has been enlightening. We learn about different perspectives, personalities, and progressions. I have also learned that we must strengthen our immune systems as we constantly evolve and travel to new places, climates, and cultures. Just as along our spiritual journey, we must strengthen our spirit, man, so that the Spirit may lead and guide us in the way we should go as we accelerate and are seated in heavenly places.

Depending on how much you work, we need to learn to be creative and innovative with our lunch and snack choices. When we go up and down, changing altitudes, we must find the best diet for flying. At least I did. My body didn't like heavy food flying, so it was primarily fruits and vegetables and a lot of water! Water is our friend in the air and on the ground!!

Just like physical water assists us in being hydrated flight attendants, the Holy Spirit helps us be hydrated for the Kingdom. Everyone needs hydration and filtration in his or her own life. I was drinking water and minding the business in my cabin! LOL! Not looking to the left nor the right but remaining focused ahead. Yes, we work as a team, which is a great skill to have in life, but being a flight attendant requires more strategic teamwork as everyone works differently, and the job itself is just different. We are one body with many parts that jointly come together to assist the pilot in assuring the safety and comfort of the passengers aboard. As flight attendants, we sometimes walk blindly into our assigned segment. We don't get to pick who we work with. Just like in the Body of

Christ, *the eye cannot say to the hand, "I don't need you, neither can the head say to the feet, "I don't need you."* – 1 Corinthians 12:21-22. We need each other as we all have something to bring to the table.

This helped me learn how to embrace different personalities, and this requires a special gift to accept who you are paired with and catch the flow of the crew you're with for the best safety practices. I'm able to do this because I put my complete trust in God, not man. Some trust in princes, but I trust in the name of the Lord! There are days when we don't see hiccups or offenses coming, so we must be flexible and patient anyhow. Sometimes, we question whether we are fit to finish a hard day. I began to understand that trouble can arise in any job setting, but we need to make it work because what we carry is greater than what we see. Furthermore, we most likely have been assigned to finish a task that seems impossible to the carnal mind. When leaning on the fleshly way of thinking, we can encounter uncertainty and become uncomfortable boldly moving forward to complete it. God tells us in His Word that He started a good work in us that will continue to perfect and complete every phase of our lives. The Holy Spirit is the copilot that comforts us and helps us navigate our next phase in life.

At the end of the day, we need to keep our hands in God's and trust the process. Trust that fear cannot win, but purpose will! We must walk daily knowing we are winning, even if our current condition challenges our position. God's thoughts are not like our thoughts, nor are His ways like our ways. We must not lean to our own understanding but trust Him in the process, although it does not make sense. My same friend that went to Chicago, during her flight, the pilot announced that they had to shift routes and go another way due to the intensity of the winds. One might think, really, in the middle of acceleration, a change occurs. Yes, this can happen. However, the critical question is whether you will trust God and shift with Him. Will you flow with the shift even when it's an abrupt shift?

Sometimes, we can fall prey when our mind does not align with our spirit. Our spirit can understand and know, but our mind sometimes fights against the truth and wants to do what it believes. What feels good or what seems right ends up wrong. When our stewardship level matures with mind, soul, and spirit (including our attitudes and wills) being brought up together, this is one example of how the true manifestation of God's will begins to flow and flow eternally. This is when nothing can trick us, not even our flesh. The only way flesh wins is if we ignore the signs because we want to be in control in some way, shape, or form. I know I am a witness to myself and others in my proximity. I used to second-guess myself about this concept. It was not until I sat and observed over and over through different individuals, family and non-family, that what we choose to do, believe, and respond to is a choice. God is a gentleman who will not force us to choose his ways, but he does warn us. *"For the Lord disciplines and corrects those whom He loves, and HE punishes every son whom He receives and welcomes to His heart"* – Hebrews 12:6 AMP.

Being a flight attendant involves risks, and we may not understand why that risk exists. Whether it's a safety risk or an unforeseen risk, we must use the safety tools we've been given, keep an open mind, and communicate clearly with the crew and customers on the plane. We don't know if the customers on the plane faced many challenges traveling that day, that week, or that month. Some may even have had to return home to a stressful, chaotic, or critical situation. We also don't know what each flight attendant may be facing personally. So, we want to make sure we are aware and sensitive on both ends, as flight attendants and customers.

Let's discuss parts of what I lived out in "The Conception of Living as a False Steward." Letting go allowed me to obtain the grace to walk in the Gospel of Peace and walk with my Shield of Faith. The Gospel of Peace, the Shod of Peace, became second nature even when I did not understand what I walked in during past battles. There was this battle between pride and faith—the spirit of pride in relation to my attitude. Even though I could see things not going well, I would attempt to still line it up with my attitude, which was out of sync, selfish, rebellious, out of control, know-it-all, and always offended about something.

A FLIGHT TO A THREE-DIMENSIONAL LEGACY

"Are We Being a Good Steward?"

I was not being a good steward. I would connect with familiar spirits when my guards were down, and my expectations were low. I would go where my underdeveloped thoughts about me would be accepted, and I would not get the urge to change, a real change. I would spend my money with people and in places that I was not supposed to, purchasing things that were not beneficial to me or my health. I was doing whatever I felt like doing, not considering the consequences. I was praying for more, wanting the increase in hopes of it shifting my situation when, in essence, it would have made it worse because, truth be told, I was not disciplined in what I already had. *"He who is faithful in a very little thing is also faithful in much, and he who is dishonest in a very little thing is also dishonest in much"* – Luke 16:10 AMP. So, to fully walk in a divine attitude, these things must be cleaned up and corrected to remain consistent in our assignments and yield, killing our flesh daily so we can become the best version of ourselves.

We once walked in deceit, and then, by God's grace, He snatched us out of it. This is when we need to start protecting what goes on in our eyes, ears, and minds. It is pertinent to protect our heads with the Helmet of Salvation and consistently spend intimate time in the Word of God, our Sword of the Spirit. One may ask how I can become a good steward in all things when what I've seen (see) most is a struggle, heartache, abuse, and despair. A good steward faithfully manages the gifts, talents, and resources entrusted to them by God. This includes material possessions, time, abilities, and the environment. Hebrews 11:6 says, *"But without faith, it is impossible to walk with God and please Him, for whoever comes near to God must necessarily believe that God exists and that He rewards those who earnestly and diligently seek Him."* we become good stewards, and this qualifies us to receive our divine allowance/inheritance.

Being a good steward means God trusts us with stewarding assets, property, people, and/or money. According to biblical principles, being a good steward is deeply rooted in the concept of responsibly managing

God's resources. The Bible emphasizes that everything we have—our time, talents, and treasures—are gifts from God, and we are entrusted with these to use them wisely and for His glory. One of the key scriptures discussing stewardship is Matthew 25:14-30, the Parable of the Talents, where servants are given money to manage while their master is away. The servants who wisely invest and increase their master's wealth are rewarded, while the one who fails to utilize his resources is reprimanded. This parable underscores the importance of productivity and accountability in stewardship.

BY FAITH and daily dying to self, we learn how to adopt the personality/attitude of Jesus Christ. Good stewardship requires an attitude of gratitude and contentment. 1 Timothy 6:6-8 mentions that *"godliness with contentment is great gain,"* suggesting that being satisfied with what we have and using it wisely is a form of honoring God. This extends beyond financial resources, including how we manage our time and skills. By recognizing that all we have is a blessing from God, we are encouraged to use our assets to serve others and further God's kingdom. This principle is reinforced in 1 Peter 4:10, which advises believers to use their gifts to serve others as faithful stewards of God's grace.

Now, let us define the words being, good, and steward as they relate to the Bible's exposition. The word Being is defined as the nature or essence of a person. With God being the head of our lives, our nature, our very being, remains pure and righteous, not because we are so good but because of the one abiding inside of us.

Being a good steward helps reduce the flaming arrows of the enemy, blocks the wiles of Satan, our adversary, by giving us the wisdom to keep our character above all else, and keeps our money, fruit of the spirit, and spiritual gifts blessed and flowing.

Adam and Eve were considered good stewards until an inquisitive mindset befell Eve's eyes, as proven in Genesis 3:6. When the woman was deceivingly convinced that the fruit of the tree was good to eat, pleasing to the eye, and desirable for gaining wisdom, she took and ate. She also gave some to her husband, who was with her, and he ate. The problem didn't lie within her consuming the fruit, but when the man, Adam, consumed the fruit, the trajectory changed as he was the head, and the instructions were laid upon him. What he was over, overpowered him through the pride of life, the inquisitive mind, and the FOMO (*fear of missing out*) in the unknown. The pride of life portion was when Adam did not take accountability for being in charge. He did not resist the temptation put before him. Instead, he entrusted the help mate that was given to him. His inquisitive mind prevailed in his accountability. Lastly, the FOMO (*fear of missing out*) seeped in when the serpent presented the temptation of knowing good and evil. Boom, that flesh rose, and as soon as Adam ate (not Eve) of the pleasant fruit, their flesh manifested for them to see, and they (Adam and Eve) were naked, or, you could say, uncovered.

This is much like a lot of the population today. When they feed the flesh what it wants, we tend to be uncovered, no longer secure in being good stewards of what we have learned and heard. Then, it becomes an internal war when our heart posture is truly revealed. Without maintaining clean hands and a pure heart posture, we get into all kinds of trouble.

Dictionary.com defines good as morally excellent, virtuous, righteous, and pious. Good cannot be present in man when his focus is misguided. This is why I believe the idea that having money is the root of all kinds of evil came into play. However, this concept is incorrect. It is not the idea of having money that is evil. It is the love of money that is the root of all evil. When you have the attitude and mindset that loves money, you can become willing to do anything for it. When we are good stewards, we protect things differently, asking for the pure eyes of the Holy One who sees good in everything He created. God made all things, and without him, nothing was made. Remember, we are to learn and grow to be good in and out of season, abasing and abounding in grace and love.

Look at the story in the next chapter of Genesis, Genesis 4. Here is a past story in a different environment dealing with a different level of stewardship. In Genesis 4, we see two brothers named Cain and Abel. They were both given the opportunity to steward the responsibility given to them. We all know the story. Cain and Abel both offered an offering to

God. However, only one of them was deemed favorable in God's eyes. One might ask, why is that? We can only make assumptions about why this happened; however, let's not miss the message within the story. Here it is. We have two people working for God, and it appears only one is recognized with favor. It is only natural for one to get emotionally angry. But honestly, ask yourself, although angry, should I act out of my emotions or seek God for a solution and guidance? As humans, we often find ourselves making rational decisions in anger. This, my friend, is a level of stewarding situations. Better yet, stewarding choices. This story teaches us that God knows our hearts' motives, even if man does not know them.

Genesis 4: 3-8 AMP says,

> "And in the course of time Cain brought to the Lord an offering of the fruit of the ground. But Abel brought [an offering of] the [finest] firstborn of his flock and the fat portions. And the Lord had respect (regard) for Abel and for his offering, but for Cain and his offering, He had no respect. So, Cain became extremely angry (indignant) and looked annoyed and hostile. And the Lord said to Cain, "Why are you so angry? And why do you look annoyed? If you do well [believing in Me and doing what is acceptable and pleasing to Me], will you not be accepted? And if you do not do well [but ignore My instruction], sin crouches at your door; its desire is for you [to overpower you], but you must master it." Cain talked with Abel, his brother [about what God had said]. And when they were [alone, working] in the field, Cain attacked Abel, his brother, and killed him."

This passage reminds me of how our attitude shifts when things don't precisely go as we expected them to or when we don't do something the Holy Spirit tells us to, resulting in consequences. We all want the Lord to favor us, but in this passage, he gives us an example of favor that deserves favor. We must heed the Lord's nudge to obey Him and fully accept His Will. God is asking, how are we stewarding our experiences? In this passage, Cain does not respond well regarding how he sees his brother. The Bible tells us, *"Be angry yet do not sin; do not let your anger cause you shame, nor allow it to last until the sun goes down"* – Ephesians 4:26AMP. Cain embodied jealousy in his heart, displayed through his disobedience of love and stewardship. There is this same attitude of conflict in families today. We sometimes do not embrace the people and/or family members God is raising this season. We tend to overlook and not celebrate the next person who receives an overflow of blessings. We do not want to be the one who says "congratulations, or you are doing a great job, to those we get too comfortable or too familiar with. We do not want to support, agree, and promote the success of others when we have not fully yielded, healed, and/or matured in Christ. We sometimes do not understand that favor is not necessarily earned through human effort alone but is seen as a manifestation of God's grace and kindness. Favor is God's divine approval, blessing, and benevolence bestowed upon us. The scriptures depict favor as a special preference or kindness that leads to protection, prosperity, and success. God positions us to receive favor. It is up to us to yield, trust, and obey. Some people may say no, this is not how it works, but in my experience, anytime God has shown me elevation, it never had a face. What do I mean? God showed me elevation, but the specifics were not disclosed. There wasn't a specific name or gender attached. Why? Romans 2:11 NLT says, *"For God does not show favoritism."* It is for whosoever believes in Him to receive the good things, the fruit of the land, which takes us back to being a good steward in all things, not just money, but relationships, friendships, and marketplace opportunities.

We are to have wealth, peace, love, joy, peace, and grace. How can we separate what the LORD encompasses? We are to walk worthy of our calling, stewarding the many gifts, talents, and skills He has entrusted us with. A part of stewardship is transparency and balance. When Jesus ministered, He ministered to everyone, not just those he liked. He answered the call and was on a mission for the Kingdom, even at the Wedding of Cana. The wedding of Cana demonstrates recognition of a need. Mary recognized there was a need when the wine ran out. A part of stewardship is recognizing when you have begun feeling drained, empty, incomplete, and need help. When we recognize this before Christ, it allows him to work within us and make us whole. As the famous William Shakespeare would say, "To thine own self be true." In hindsight, we must recognize and believe that Jesus imparted the necessary seeds in us. He planted the seeds of spiritual riches and wealth in us before we even thought about being born, which had to be cultivated by faith to even begin to tap into being good stewards with wholesome attitudes. By accepting His Will, we start to walk in our full inheritance of wealth manifested in physical wealth. We have to see that seedtime and harvest. Genesis 8:22 states, *"While the earth remaineth, seedtime and harvest, and cold and heat, and summer and winter, and day and night shall not cease."* So, seedtime and harvest will always remain.

A Divine attitude will find ways to sow seeds consistently as God directs. It is by Faith that we realize our condition but stand up and accept our position in the kingdom. This is not a human flow but a God flow. When we grasp a hold of our attitude so that it is not swayed with every wind and doctrine, we become ready for acceleration and divine elevation. A divine attitude consists of love and mercy. Love means grace, and mercy is continuous forgiveness. Then, when we release these concepts, we shift people and atmosphere. Having a divine attitude is a protected understanding that we are no longer on the wrong path. We begin to see things shift, the old proclivities start to fade, the newness of life rises, and we inhabit our territory and rightful space. Our job to possess our divine attitude is a space that thrusts us into who we are to become. It is the ability to see clearly who we are and who we are without waiting for others to confirm or agree with us.

To walk in a divine attitude completely, we must accept the Holy Spirit and allow the Holy Spirit to dwell inside us as we take our position in Him (GOD). We can then walk in a divine attitude that we know we belong to Jesus and he to us as we continue in the faith in the position God gave us. Our position grows to maturity, and our attitude links with God as our ultimate source. When we understand that no man can do what God can, we begin to be succinct in thinking and processing through life. This prepares us for shifts and redirections that life requires when we are in

God. When we are in God, we must lay down our perceptions, misunderstandings, and any wrong thinking that may try to come in and snuff out the plans of God. It is by Faith that we accept our position in the kingdom. This is not a human flow but a God flow. You know your mindset has shifted when you start observing differently and doing things with love and intentionality. Are you living with complete love and truth coupled with intentionality? Let us love one another, for love comes from God. Whoever does not love does not know God because God is love. God lives in us by loving one another, and his love is made complete each day we connect intimately with Him.

In the closing of Section 1, there is no fear in love. But perfect love drives out fear (anxiety) because it is punished. The one who fears is not made perfect in love. Now, let's do our CLUES (questions) before we proceed to Section 3, Divine Assembly.

Divine Attitude Discussion

1. How can you improve your divine attitude after reading this section?

   _____
   _____
   _____
   _____
   _____
   _____
   _____

2. How do you process situations?

   _____
   _____
   _____
   _____
   _____
   _____
   _____

3. Take inventory of the stewardship of every area of your life. What area(s) would you say you could steward better? What area(s) can you say you have been a faithful steward?

_____

_____

_____

_____

_____

_____

_____

4. Do you find yourself not stewarding areas well? Ask God to instruct and guide you on how to do better.

_____

_____

_____

_____

_____

_____

_____

5. Do you reevaluate your circle consistently as you elevate in life? Has anything changed? If so, how?

_____

_____

_____

_____

_____

_____

Note—These are self-evaluation questions to assist you in building and strengthening this area of your life. It is essential to take the necessary steps and learn this skill before proceeding to this flight's second leg.

Section 3

DIVINE ASSEMBLY

Quote - " For it is at the appointed time that we walk into our divine foreknowledge, provisional insight, and wealth transfers. Gathered in the divine assembly, we are united by a higher purpose, where every soul is a unique thread woven into the tapestry of the universe, creating a masterpiece of love, wisdom, and strength."

This section will discuss some key aspects of the divine building of others and the divine assembly from the corporate and kingdom standpoints, with a particular focus on the application of religious principles to corporate leadership.

A divine assembly transcends the typical corporate gathering. It is a harmonious congregation marked by a profound sense of unity. This unity is not just a concept but a reality that binds us all together, giving us a shared purpose and strategic alignment. The participants, ideally in sync, work towards the common goal of the company's prosperity, acting with a level of wisdom and foresight that one might attribute to a 'divine' group. This interpretation unveils a concept of an elite, highly effective, and purpose-driven gathering of key individuals within a company working together.

The concept of a divine assembly underscores the biblical theme of God's sovereignty and the organized structure of the heavenly realm. It illustrates that God's governance extends beyond the earthly sphere and involves a complex hierarchy of spiritual beings. This notion reinforces the idea of a well-ordered cosmos where every entity, whether human or celestial, operates under the divine authority and wisdom of God. Just as the word reminds us in Eph 4:11-16 input version (AMP)

> *"And [His gifts to the church were varied and] He Himself appointed some as apostles [special messengers, representatives], some as prophets [who speak a new message from God to the people], some as evangelists [who spread the good news of salvation], and some as pastors and teachers [to shepherd and guide and instruct], [and He did this] to fully equip and perfect the saints (God's people) for works of service, to build up the body of Christ [the church]; until we all reach oneness in the faith and in the knowledge of the Son of God, [growing spiritually] to become a mature believer, reaching to the measure of the fullness of Christ [manifesting His spiritual completeness and exercising our spiritual gifts in unity]. So that we are no longer children [spiritually immature], tossed back and forth [like ships on a*

stormy sea] and carried about by every wind of [shifting] doctrine, by the cunning and trickery of [unscrupulous] men, by the deceitful scheming of people ready to do anything [for personal profit]. But speaking the truth in love [in all things—both our speech and our lives expressing His truth], let us grow up in all things into Him [following His example], who is the Head—Christ. From Him the whole body [the church, in all its various parts], joined and knitted firmly together by what every joint supplies, when each part is working properly, causes the body to grow and mature, building itself up in [unselfish] love."

Divine Building

Building others requires leadership qualities such as selfless dedication, strong intentions, and effective execution. It's almost like community development or a not-for-profit organizational approach. So, as a community of the kingdom, just like our Father God, we should have an obligation to plant the necessary seeds to help others peak maturity on all levels. 1 Corinthians 3:6-8AMP demonstrates the process of the planter, waterer, and the increase.

"I planted, Apollos watered, but God [all the while] was causing the growth. So, neither is the one who plants nor the one who waters anything, but [only] God who causes the growth. He who plants and he who waters are one [in importance and esteem, working toward the same purpose]; but each will receive his own reward according to his own labor."

Being a planter signifies a role that involves spreading and nurturing the seeds of faith and the teachings of God. Being a planter is characterized by patience and diligence. Just as a farmer must carefully prepare the soil, plant the seeds, and tend to them while waiting for the harvest, a spiritual planter must be committed to sharing the message of faith, even when immediate results are not visible. This involves teaching, witnessing, and living out one's faith in a manner that can inspire and encourage others. It underscores the importance of perseverance and trust in divine timing.

Furthermore, being a planter involves collaboration and community. The biblical concept of planting is not a solitary endeavor; it often involves working together with others who may contribute different skills and gifts to the process. Just as Paul and Apollos had distinct roles, the modern-day faith community also functions best when individuals work together, each playing their part in nurturing and growing the faith of the community. This cooperative effort reflects the larger body of Christ and highlights the interconnectedness and interdependence of its members.

Being a waterer signifies a role that involves nurturing, facilitating growth, and supporting the spiritual development of others. A waterer is someone who contributes to the spiritual nourishment of others. This could be through teaching, encouragement, acts of kindness, or simply being supportive in someone's life. The act of watering implies ongoing care and attention, helping others to flourish in their faith.

Furthermore, being a waterer can also be seen as a collaborative effort within the community. Just as plants need both planting and watering to grow, spiritual growth often requires the combined efforts of multiple people. This underscores the importance of community and the interdependent nature of spiritual development. Each person's contribution, whether planting seeds of faith or nurturing those seeds, is valuable in God's overall plan. Thus, to be a waterer biblically is to be an active participant in the growth and encouragement of others, recognizing that while our efforts are important, it is ultimately God who brings about true spiritual growth.

What does this have to do with my flight? I'm glad that you asked. Being a flight attendant has given me the opportunity to plant seeds as I serve. It made me realize the importance of my demeanor and actions toward others, including the ones that have wronged me. I thank God daily for trusting me with this role. I enjoy speaking the language of others, delivering the good news, and planting seeds of joy, peace, kindness, and love amongst my teammates and every customer who flies. Many times,

God will position us in the corporate world to not only enhance and gain new skills but also to plant kingdom seeds in the lives of others and, in some cases, water the seeds that have already been planted. Ask yourself, in this season of your life, what is God having you to do? Are you a planter or a waterer?

It's just a matter of time. Change will come in true divine assembly! There are multiple blessings available in the divine building. Things will happen so fast you won't be able to keep up; everything is multiplying because of our faithfulness and obedience. Overflow has overshadowed us, a shower of blessings. It's about what God wants corporately, so as we ask him for things, ensure there is a valid kingdom reason, rule, or principle to back the ASKS. We can't think every release is a God release without us first doing as Matthew 6:33 instructs, seeking first the kingdom so that all can be added. This means that as believers, we are to put God's will and values at the forefront of our lives. To seek first the kingdom means to focus on living according to the principles and values that Jesus taught. This includes loving others, practicing kindness, pursuing justice, and maintaining integrity in all aspects of life. It emphasizes the importance of a personal relationship with God and living in a way that reflects His love and righteousness. By doing so, as believers, we trust that God will take care of our material needs and concerns.

In a broader sense, this concept can also be interpreted as prioritizing what is truly important in life. It calls for a shift from a self-centered or materialistic focus to a more altruistic and spiritually-centered approach. By embodying compassion, humility, and faith, we can contribute positively to our communities and the world around us.

A FLIGHT TO A THREE-DIMENSIONAL LEGACY

Cross-Check Analysis

"Cross-check" is usually used before "doors-to-arrival," but not always. It's just a signal that flight attendants should watch and check the work of their colleagues to ensure that everything is locked and armed safely."

In the flight attendant world, we are called to cross-checks to prepare others for their journey to their next place. What is a cross-check? It is a procedure to ensure the safety and security of the aircraft, its passengers, and crew members. This is done before takeoff and landing to verify that all safety protocols and equipment are correctly in place. This includes confirming doors are properly armed or disarmed, ensuring that emergency exits are unobstructed, and verifying that seatbelts are fastened and tray tables are stowed.

In 1 Corinthians 3, God tells us that we are His fellow workers who were given grace to prepare for our task like a skillful master builder. He desires for us to build on the already laid foundation, which is Jesus Christ. He also says that we are His cultivated field, garden, vineyard, and building. He forewarns us in verse 13 that our work will be tested. He says, *"each one's work will be clearly shown [for what it is]; for the day [of judgment] will disclose it, because it is to be revealed with fire, and the fire will test the quality and character and worth of each person's work."* Like a cross-check, God performs a cross-check analysis before transitioning us to our next place. This is to assure the safety of our hearts, minds, spirits, and souls. Oxford Languages defines analysis as a detailed examination of the elements or structure of something. The seeds that we plant shall be examined(tested). The variety of seeds being planted is demonstrated in the parable of the Sower.

> *"A farmer went out to sow his seed. As he was scattering the seed, some fell along the path, and the birds came and ate it up. Some fell on rocky places, where it did not have much soil. It sprang up quickly, because the soil was shallow. But when the sun came up,*

the plants were scorched, and they withered because they had no root. Other seed fell among thorns, which grew up and choked the plants. Still other seed fell on good soil, where it produced a crop—a hundred, sixty or thirty times what was sown." – Matthew 13:3-7NIV.

When sowing seeds, we must cross-check every seed with the Father to ensure that everything is locked and armed safely before being released. Cross-Check the delivery of the seed. What is the condition of your mindset? What is your heart posture? What is your true purpose? Just as we are to ensure that emergency exits are unobstructed, we are to ensure that seed planting is unobstructed. There are some things we cannot help or prevent, but as long as we know we have followed the instructions of the Father in the planting process, we must trust the Father to take care of the rest.

Knowing You and Your Audience

"Do you not know and understand that you [the church] are the temple of God and that the Spirit of God dwells [permanently] in you [collectively and individually]? If anyone destroys the temple of God [corrupting it with false doctrine], God will destroy the destroyer; for the temple of God is holy (sacred), and that is what you are." – 1 Corinthians 3:16-17AMP

Divine Building is a shadow type of community service and the village of an open Heaven. Some people escape home training or make it of no effect in their lives, tending to lean on their own understanding. In the book of Judges, the people were without a king and were left to do what was right in their own eyes. Can you imagine living in today's world without governmental officials? It would be chaotic beyond chaotic as we all have our own way of thinking and sometimes believe our thinking is right. God does things in decency and in order, which is why *"He gave some apostles, and some prophets, and some evangelists, and some pastors and teachers for the perfecting of the saints for the work of the ministry for the edifying of the body of Christ"*- Ephesians 4:11-12 KJV.

God instructed Jeremiah to uproot and tear down, destroy and overthrow, build and plant. In order for something to be rebuilt, it must first go through the gutting out process that requires uprooting and tearing down the old, destroying and overthrowing one's mindset, and making room for a renewed mind to be transformed and planted.

Divine building assists others in growing up in Christ. The famous Paul demonstrates this in the book of Colossians. Paul never stopped praying for the people and asked God to fill them with knowledge of his will through all the wisdom and understanding that the Spirit gives. He wanted them to live a life worthy of the Lord and bear fruit in every good work. He desired for them to continually grow in the knowledge of God, being strengthened with all power according to God's glorious might so that they may have great endurance and patience. In the end, he wanted them to gain the attitude of giving joyful thanks to the Father, who is the ultimate qualifier to position you to share in the inheritance of his holy people in the kingdom of light. - Colossians 1:9-12 NIV We have to get to a place of not gatekeeping but instead sharing the wisdom given to us with others. God wants us to edify and build one another and not become selfish in our ways, not wanting the next person to grow quickly. Psalms 133 says it is good when kingdom brethren dwell together in unity.

Divine building provides the necessary tools for others to come into their purpose in Christ, as we need the Holy Spirit to dwell, navigate, guide, and transfer strategies. Granted, divine building can also benefit our missions and goals. However, the foundation is to incorporate others and collaborate rather than compete. When we build together, we win, grow, and mature faster. As God said in Genesis, "It is not good for man to be alone."

A friend once told me, "God will surround you with people where you are headed and not where you are." We must maintain a positive attitude and not become intimidated when surrounded by those who are smarter or more advanced than we are. Look at it from the perspective of being stretched beyond our own visible capacity. Just as we are the missing piece to someone else's puzzle, God will surround us with others who carry what we need to complete the mission or vision. Say this with me, "I am not a problem but a solution!" Apostle Sammy C. Smith said it this way, "God created you to be a solution to a problem. If you're not a solution, you have become a part of the problem."

You may ask, "How do you know that you have entered a relationship level of building? When you get to the mindset that not everyone is out to get you, it eliminates the barriers of non-trust and non-commitment. One must first understand that everyone and everything has a purpose in their life. It is a matter of discovering what that purpose may be. There is a time, a place, and a season for everything. Recognizing the season, place, and time helps avoid disappointment when it does not go as planned. A relationship, whether a friendship, family member, co-worker or even someone you are interested in, involves more than one person willing to become vulnerable with the other. Just as Adam and Eve were naked in the garden demonstrating open vulnerability, once they gained the knowledge of how vulnerable they were, they went into hiding, trying to cover themselves. How many people do you know cover up their vulnerability in fear of being hurt or taken advantage of?

I was listening to a podcast one day, and they talked about building a house of relationships. They said, "The foundation of this house was connectivity plus God; the frame was communication plus God; the windows were built from floor to ceiling, representing awareness plus God; the doors were God, and the roof was love, which is God." If you pay close attention, every section and part of building the house of a relationship incorporates God. This is because "what God put together, no man can part." The first part of every relationship is connectivity. God will put something or someone in place to make the connection. Once the connection is made, then communication will follow. Communication is a vital part of every relationship. Where there is no communication, there is no relationship. In communication, you continue to discover and build each other up. This falls into awareness. One must be aware of their trigger points and also where they are physically, mentally, emotionally, and spiritually. This requires one to be true to one's self. Communication also assists with building the roof of the relationship, which is love. Love is being built on an ongoing basis, just as God continually communicates with us. This is how we should relationally build others, not based on a person's current condition but on future position.

Have you had an anointed person pray with and over you and agree to tarry until something breaks? If not, I pray you do. There is nothing like it. We may experience few or many deliverance sessions, and these moments count as deliverance sessions, where your mind shifts up, and you don't leave there the way you came. You are wiser and have obtained more clarity. However, one must not stop at the place of deliverance. One must be willing to move forward toward the journey of development. Apostle Sammy C. Smith said, "A person can be delivered but not developed." What does this mean?

Delivered means to set free, to draw out, or to give up or hand over. When we understand that being delivered ends up being a model for someone else to track or follow, we are then able to help others be set free, drawn out, and blessed through their obedience. Part of being delivered is understanding and teaching others that sacrificial giving of your time, money, and intelligence is a form of worship unto God. Being delivered allows us to plant the seeds, take the necessary steps, and form the necessary mindset to track with God and become his pure vessel that is submitted to advancing the kingdom of God. Being delivered proves what the word says about all falling short and that all have been given the opportunity to manifest our inheritance on earth. Our inheritance is an extension of our legacy and influence in the world, where we are able to defeat generational trauma and subtract backlashes. Through our obedience, the Lord will deliver it all unto our hands, and it will have to become subject to what we speak. This is why we must be mindful of what we say, as the power is in our tongue to speak life or death. When filled with the word, it increases the process of deliverance, revealing the level of our faith. It incites the celebration and the recovery of life and provides words of knowledge coupled with wisdom and understanding. So, one may say that incite is not the appropriate word, but remember, in the preface or introduction, we spoke about words having earthly wisdom or heavenly wisdom. Incite, in the world's meaning, is viewed as not good; however, in the word of God, incite means to stir up, encourage, or invoke. True deliverance circumcises our ear gates to receive divine instructions, posturing us for healing and complete restoration.

Developed means that we are being released in stages as every detail is being directly proportioned in the time it is to be released. When we build others, it is important that we explain that everything will not be downloaded at one time but at its appointed time. Transparency must be at the forefront of development as it explains how and why we must coordinate a thing and how we learn to facilitate what we have been given. Just like a farmer who is given seeds to plant, he starts by tilling the dirt and breaking up the fallow ground so that he may plant the necessary seeds in the appropriate places so that they may sprout in the ordained places. Kingdom keys can be released when we grow past the things we once loved in our flesh and teach people to reach for noble and pure things.

When combining the two processes, think of it this way: Deliverance is the tilling process of fallow ground, and development is the seeds being planted in their rightful place to position you in alignment with the Will of God.

In 1 Corinthians 14:4, the apostle Paul says something amazing: "He who prophesies builds up the church." Prophesying is not merely foretelling the future but mainly speaking for Christ, speaking forth Christ, and speaking Christ into others to encourage, edify, admonish, and exhort the building up of the church as we are the church. In divine building, you will be planted in a network of people who help you excel in every area: those areas that you couldn't fight by yourself, those areas that you were ashamed of, those areas of opportunity that you wouldn't have ever suspected entering into. The network is designed to establish success and push you to thrive mentally before it manifests itself physically. The saying says, "You have to see yourself there first before you even get there." This is the purpose of God surrounding you with people where you're going and not where you are. These types of networks of people will be supported and will support you! What a great feeling to experience during your transition up.

God provided a network that entails the fivefold ministry to expose you to opportunities you couldn't see alone. He also opens relational opportunities in the marketplace community. Everything we do for God is relevant to the Kingdom and reveals even more about how to operate and apply the principles of the Kingdom here on Earth. This community incorporates your business, work, community activities, or sports. However, before getting to the stage of exposure, one must be detoxed frequently, resting in the presence of God. It is important as we build others up.

The Apostle Paul said, "To live is Christ, and to die is gain."- Philippians 1:21. He then says that "he dies daily."-1Corinthians 15:31. From the perspective of being a mindset coach, it is important to watch our emotions and recharge appropriately each day. Things happen to us each day that are out of our control, as we cannot control people. We need to get our rest each day, and we should emotionally detox each day as well.

As you divinely accelerate, we need to check our circle and keep a healthy mindset and perception as we engage and do business. Maintaining close attention to our filters(mouth) and personal space (boundaries and circles) as we ascend into different dimensions is important. One indicator that we may need to Detox and Rest is if we get upset too quickly with strangers. This is a sign that we need to detox our emotions. Oxford defines detox as a period of time when one rids the body of unhealthy substances or people, places, and things.

Hearing the flesh is different from hearing the Holy Spirit. For example, our flesh may want to proceed with a thing, but the Holy Spirit warns us and guides us in dealing with situations and/or people. So, please pay attention, as sometimes there are indicators that we need to proceed with caution.

A FLIGHT TO A THREE-DIMENSIONAL LEGACY

Divine Intervention: We are the Students First

King Solomon wrote, "*Let the wise hear and increase in learning, and the one who understands obtain guidance*" (Proverbs 1:5). This verse emphasizes the principle of remaining teachable. A student can develop and become a teacher, but a teacher never stops being a student. The famous John C. Maxwell wrote in his book "The 21 Irrefutable Laws of Leadership" the first principle of leadership, which was the law of the lid. The concept of this law was to bring recognition to the capping abilities of one's potential. One can only go as far as they allow themselves to go. One must gain the ability to break through barriers by remaining teachable, which will enable them to continue growing and thriving.

Divine intervention is a powerful force, a beacon of hope that guides us towards self-improvement. It illuminates the areas of our conduct and behaviors that need change, helping us understand how our past actions may have hindered our growth and that of others. This intervention is not a punishment, but a necessary step towards accountability and growth. It's a hopeful message that even in our darkest moments, there's a path to redemption.

"There is a Necessary Purge!"

May the real teachers of my foundation please stand up. Don't hide behind someone you think may be more enlightened or appear to have more influence or head knowledge. Let's challenge ourselves to understand the Word better to increase the body in clarity, knowledge, wisdom, and stature, leading people to Jesus! Let our motivation not be a title. Lord, help us as we flow in scriptural truths.

When God ordains you, your position in Him is secure, higher than any title man can give. No man can take an ordination, but if man gives it and God hasn't confirmed it first or confirmed it at all, the title that man gives can be rescinded by man's hand. This is a comforting truth, a reminder that our spiritual journey is not dependent on human validation, but on God's divine ordination. When God truly sends you, no devil in hell can move you or stop you from flowing in the things of God; even you can't shake it when God brands you for greatness. This is a message of security and confidence, a reassurance that our spiritual journey is guided by a higher power, and no earthly force can deter us from our path.

The Apostle John wrote, *"He cuts off every branch in me that bears no fruit, while every branch that does bear fruit he prunes so that it will be even more fruitful"* (John 15:2). In this metaphor, Jesus is the vine, the source of our spiritual nourishment and strength, and His followers are the branches, the ones which draw from His divine power. The principle conveyed here is one of spiritual growth and productivity. The 'cutting off' of unfruitful branches represents the removal of those aspects of a person's life that do not contribute to spiritual growth or bear positive outcomes. This could pertain to harmful habits, negative influences, or anything that detracts from a follower's spiritual journey. By removing these unproductive elements, a person is given the opportunity to focus on what truly matters and grow in their faith. The pruning/purging process encourages healthy growth. In a spiritual context, this means that even those who are already bearing fruit- demonstrating positive qualities and good deeds- undergo a process of refinement. This pruning/purging can be seen as life's challenges and trials that, while difficult, help to strengthen and deepen a person's faith, making them even more fruitful in their spiritual journey. As believers, we have been given the opportunity of continuous growth and the transformative power of removing the negative to make way for the positive. As the famous Paul wrote, "The old life is gone; a new life emerges" (2 Corinthians 5:17).

We must make sure we don't treat our gifts and fruits as common. The chosen are being called up to the Mount of Transfiguration. When we come down, we are assigned new territories and a new name with a new identity. Glory to God. "His feet were bruised by strong shackles, and his soul was held by iron." Our feet resemble our peace. Sometimes in life, what God initially puts in us gets tainted, our souls are bruised, and we become mentally captive and can't break free. It's something when a person is physically free but mentally bound in adversity. This person was me. I have been ordained in the faith, bruised and bleeding. God broke me down to nothing and refined me to something even greater. God is healing and filling us with joy and virtue so that people can be free, living the life He predestined for us to live. It is not our job to present ourselves but for God to present us well. Psalms 105:18-19 TPT states, *"God's promise to Joseph purged his character until it was time for his dreams to come true."* WOW!!! We must first go through a purging process to make room for the new. When I read this, it reminded me of Luke 5:37, which says, *"And no one pours new wine into old wineskins. Otherwise, the new wine will burst the skins; the wine will run out, and the wineskins will be ruined."* It's like the saying, "You can't expect old keys to be able to open new doors." I had a friend who had to change the locks on the doors in her home. All of the locks were identical in style; however, the structure of the key was shaped differently. Before realizing this, she tried to use an old key to unlock the door. It was able to be inserted into the keylock; however, it was not able to turn. Why? Because it was the wrong key. When she used the new key, the door unlocked with ease. It was then that she compared the two keys and noticed there was a restructuring of keys. During the purging process, God is restructuring your keys, giving you full access to the things of the Kingdom with ease.

As we continue our walk with God, some necessary purges, deliverance, and development need to take place. The purging is necessary because the old and the new are disjointed and don't mix.
God is the one who draws, meaning he sends for his elect. The scripture Psalms 105:20-21 TPT says

> *"Eventually, the king of Egypt sent for him, setting him free at last. Then Joseph was put in charge of everything under the king; he became the master of the palace over all the royal possessions."*

This means that once we embrace our callings and follow suit, being truly in alignment, everything else falls into place. Wealth is produced by being in sync with God, as proven in Psalm 105:24 TPT, which says, *"God made them very fruitful, and they multiplied incredibly until they were greater in number than those who ruled them."*

The Process

As we build, it is more effective if we share the process as we explain the necessary purge that takes place. Elder John wrote, *"They triumphed over him by the blood of the Lamb and by the word of their testimony"* (Revelation 12:11). In our process, we learn how to cope and categorize things, but this only works as a temporary band-aid.

You may say, "What are you talking about?" When going through the purging process, I found myself tucking things in compartments to continue to move forward, which only worked for a season. After that season, those things started to come out of my pores and speech in the form of unfiltered anger, rejection, hardened hearts, envy, and jealousy. So, in this season, I stress the importance of not running from the "REAL"(**R**edeemed **E**ternal **A**bundant **L**ove) process. As *"love covers the multitude of sin"* (1 Peter 4:8). I stress the importance of peeling back one layer at a time to get to the root of unhealthy coping mechanisms and resolve the blurred lines of deficiencies. If you don't know how to resolve the lines, engage God. His line upon line, his precept upon precept, will not steer you in the wrong direction. Ask the LORD for wisdom. He will give you the wisdom to bear with yourself or others or give you a way of escape. It is our choice to take it or stay in bondage.

We must believe that God is a rewarder of those who diligently seek him as He will present opportunities for us to cultivate and come back stronger than ever. Today, I urge you not to give up on your process, wherever you are, as on the other side of the process is divine justice and recompense for your son and your daughter. What we have overcome is not for naught. I decree and declare that your confidence in God shall be established.

A FLIGHT TO A THREE-DIMENSIONAL LEGACY

Divine Assembly- Corporate Settings

In corporate settings, we must be good with who we are, who God made us to be, what God has allowed us to do, and how God has allowed tests. By the time we reach consistency in corporate divine assembly settings, we have been through enough wind and storms to unlock some kingdom keys. You may ask, what are Kingdom Keys? Kingdom Keys are access points of elevation in which you have been prepared to access, own, and appropriate with the wisdom of God.

Kingdom Keys help us mature and help others recognize how to unlock their keys to destiny. At this point, we have been through enough things that we may even know how to get a prayer through. One indication that we are ready for divine corporate settings is being able to be vulnerable enough to share an intimate language with the LORD to not only bless you but also bless others to which you are connected. There are a few components we will discuss that are a part of unlocking Kingdom keys: Prayer, Worship, and Relationship.

Learning how to pray about everything is key. There was a method or steps that have been imparted to me by various Kingdom Leaders, and this method of prayer has never let God or me down. It is the formula called ACTSI, which is Adoring God for who He is, what He has done, and what He shall do; Confessing to God that we all have fallen short of the Glory of God and the fact that we have failed people as well; Thanking God for all the ways He has made and continues to make; Supplication unto God, which is asking for help to finish the race, assignment, and more; then I, which is Intercession, the interceding of the needs of others.

Secondly, learn how to create a personal worship experience before entering a corporate setting. Your Worship Experience matters as it helps to take the corporate body up each time you dwell together corporately. Yes, come with your own fire and your own personal dedication to God to edify the body of Christ. I can hear Apostle Antwain Braggs admonishing the body to come with your own Amens and to come with your own

Hallelujahs inside of you so no one will have to pry and pull worship out of you.

To function well in corporate settings, there is an underlying governance and assembly that I had to first cultivate inside of myself. I had to understand that a personal relationship with Christ is needed. Yes, a personal relationship with Christ and thus learning how to commune with him daily through prayer, meditation, and listening. Not only that, but in each session, we spend with the Holy Spirit, we are fully yielding our heart and whatever it contains. Then, understand that we must have faith in GOD, knowing He knows what to do with it, exactly how to mend it, process it, bend it, and caress it. Especially in corporate settings, it should be unto the Lord first, which will keep us in line with individual growth and maturity. We begin to learn excellency, and our hearts remain pure, and our hands remain clean. *"Who shall ascend into the hill of the Lord? or who shall stand in his holy place? "He that hath clean hands, and a pure heart, who hath not lifted up his soul unto vanity, nor sworn deceitfully"* (Psalm 24:3–4). We can wash our hands but still have not fully allowed God to cleanse our hearts. God is the only one who can see our hearts, so one can seem one way going through the motions, but God is the only one who can discern the heart's motives. As the famous Samuel wrote, *"Do not look at his appearance or at his physical stature…The Lord does not see as man sees; for man looks at the outward appearance, but the Lord looks at the heart"* (1 Samuel 16:7).

In addition, in the clergy and corporate settings, we must remain consistent in our devotion to God, bringing us into more accountability in our assigned spaces. We also learn how to apply and maintain a balance between the ministry and our personal life. We begin to learn how to ask for wisdom and discernment, often finding ourselves in a state of repentance. James said, *"If any of you lacks wisdom, you should ask God, who gives generously to all without finding fault, and it will be given to you"* (James 1:5). Possessing the fruit of the spirit is even more pertinent in this type of setting as God is Spirit. The multiplying process of the fruit we carry incorporates building and edifying each other and returning to the foundation of YES(Yield, Edify, Spirit). When we yield, His Spirit enlightens us to obtain His fruit.

We must detox our emotions and spirits before entering these corporate sessions, corporate prayer, and even our weekly church services and places of worship. The Apostle John tells us we must worship God in spirit and truth. This way, God can do his great work, Kairos work, when you and I are out of His way. I believe we will see miracles. I believe we would see more people attending church, expecting multiple shifts and changes. These changes don't come alone. They come with divine strategies and divine opportunities to push God's mission. This confirms what fuels assembly corporately. I have experienced it where a person comes in one way, and because there was enough of God's remnant in the building with the Holy Spirit working in them, some individuals did not leave out the way they came in. They will never return to the state in which they came in.

Let me admonish the Body of Christ. It's bigger than us. We are talking of a continuous personal relationship with God. So, it's not enough to attend weekly services on Sunday and even Wednesday night Bible study but to have the desire to study His word daily. Joshua tells us to meditate on His Word day and night(Joshua 1:8). Just us and him, him and us. 1 Corinthians 12 MSG version ministers to us how each joint in the body supplies and many more things. We are to find ourselves in scripture., and *"do our best to present ourselves to God as one approved, a worker who does not need to be ashamed and who correctly handles the word of truth"* (2 Timothy 2:15).

In a corporate setting, God wants us to use our intelligence, acknowledging Him in all of our ways so that He may direct our paths. God says, "He didn't ask us to understand. He asked us to trust Him and obey." It is not for us to lean to our own understanding but to seek Him for wisdom in any area we feel we lack. God's various ministries are carried out everywhere, but they all originate in God's Spirit. He decides who gets what and when. I want you to think about how all this makes you more significant, not less. How can the leg say to the thigh it doesn't need it? We could look at this physiologically and spiritually. The word says in Hebrews 10:25, *"Not forsaking the assembling of ourselves together, as the manner of some is but exhorting one another: and so much the more, as ye see the day approaching."*

In other words, we need each other. We come together so that no one in the Kingdom of God begins to rely on themselves to run the race alone. Sometimes in our lives, we become weak and need other kingdom people to pray, speak, or intercede on our behalf. There are many blessings within the corporate setting, and there is much more strength and grace to fight together with the body than standing up to an evil regiment for which you have no training. This is why I am blessed to have received and still receive ministry training. Ministry training strengthens our cores by teaching us how to handle bigger pressures and bigger challenges so that we won't ever shrink back to things that once had us bound.

We must be able to "Reach One Teach One," remaining teachable, being students, being open to learning, and flowing together. The word tells us to bear one with another. We must ensure that our brothers and sisters acknowledge and accept the Holy Spirit.

In corporate settings, we need to follow the Holy Spirit, being led at all times by Him. Corporate settings are our training ground and position us to be fishermen of men. This is where we find out what we have been graced for and who we are to mentor or be mentored by. Further, in corporate settings, we find our midwives. We find out about the core of individuals because the Holy Spirit, the glory, shines light on things that need to be changed, modified, and implemented. Holy Spirit, in corporate settings, teaches us how to agree with our brother even if we disagree honestly. As the saying says, "We agree to disagree." No one should be left without comfort, direction, guidance, or growth. It reveals to us the levels of where people are. As a corporate body, we must govern and cover one another as we continue to grow and mature.

Grace For the Race

So, in a corporate setting, we must stop, think, and show forth mercy. Let me expound. We must show compassion and grace for others in individual settings, but we must show forth mercy in corporate. We can't judge someone else's race, nor can we judge the pace at which they are going. James says,

> *"Don't speak evil against each other. If you criticize and judge each other, then you are criticizing and judging God's law. God alone, who gave the law, is the Judge. He alone has the power to save or to destroy. So, what right do you have to judge your neighbor?"*- James 4:11-12 NLT

We must be careful of how we handle others. God sometimes allows us to see others' flaws so that we may pray for them in times of struggle and provide them with the necessary tools to persevere and endure what we overcame by God's grace. If he did it for us, he could also do it for them. In corporate settings, you learn that you will face some challenges that develop and mature you. But we must *"press on to reach the end of the race and receive the heavenly prize for which God, through Christ Jesus, is calling us."*-Philippians 3:14 NLT.

You may ask, what are some ways we divinely build others?

1. By praying for God's perfect Will over others
2. By listening with empathy
3. By using our gifts and callings to provide resources for others to continue to ascend
4. By obeying God's instructions, construction, and allowing the reconstruction of our plans, we will be established on a firm footing.
5. By genuinely helping and believing in others.

In closing this section, Divine Assembly, I want to share with you a few ingredients that have helped me to further understand how to continue building myself and others.

A Prophetess sister and friend of mine once shared a live performance, and the speaker, who was also a Prophetess, confirmed that you can receive a personal move off a corporate word! So, corporate settings with corporate praise, prayer, and worship are vital and can end up being extended access to lifelines.

Apostle Amos Benefield says it's best that we understand our functionality in the body of believers. He goes deeper and explains that functionality is a quantity or state of being functional. Understanding our functionalities and properly stewarding the gifts will better equip us to serve in our God-given purposes. It is urgent that we learn how to serve in the body of Christ in our original God-given purpose. Every function has a purpose. Every purpose has two things: it has capacity, and it has jurisdiction. He explains this is why the body can appear shipwrecked because people take on roles that they do not have the capacity for. The true takeaway from this section is to be careful in thinking that the only people that God sends to you will be willing to accept the revelation and directions shared. Beloved, God can use anybody to help you move the needle to the next level. It may not always come from someone or something familiar. This is how we miss the move of God, thinking that no one but the ones that we approve of can speak into our lives or provide necessary revelation to shift the trajectory of our lives.

Section 3 - Divine Assembly Questions

Within the context of Divine Building, we must forget the past and push forward to what lies ahead of us. This means forgiving all that you feel may have wronged you, talked about you, misguided you, mishandled you, etc., to get to a place where you accept being in full relationship with God. We must stop seeking approval from people and work on pleasing God in all ways, in all forms.

1. What does divine assembly mean to you?

_____

_____

_____

_____

_____

_____

_____

2. Do you believe that you have been sent to divine builders? Why or why not?

_____

_____

_____

_____

_____

_____

_____

3. Do you find yourself building others? Why or why not?

_____

_____

_____

_____

_____

_____

_____

4. Have you accepted divine intervention before? Were you aware that it was an intervention, or did you look at it as a correction?

_____

_____

_____

_____

_____

_____

_____

5. Do you see yourself whole and healed? Why or why not? If not, list a few steps that you can begin with to make the changes needed to live a full life.

_____

_____

_____

_____

_____

_____

_____

6. Where do you see yourself in the kingdom community within the next two years? Let us set short-term and long-term goals to grow and remain consistent in God's work.

_____

_____

_____

_____

_____

_____

_____

Section 4

DIVINE ACCELERATION

Quote - " For the vision is yet for an appointed time; but at the end, it shall speak, and not lie; though it tarry, wait for it; because it will surely come, it will not tarry"
-Habakkuk 2:3

Welcome to the Section 4 segment of your flight. I am your Flight attendant and midwife in this section. We have ascended 30,000 feet in altitude into higher realms of business, higher levels of thinking, finance, and relationships. All this while we trust, believe, and move in God! Remember, God is a God of movement and order. Our acceleration is a sign of us being fully restored in God's divine plan.

Genesis 1 starts with God in action. He created the earth, then hovered, and his face moved upon the deep. He was, is, and is ever yet moving. His continuous movement, His active presence, propels us forward, not dwelling on what happened or where we are but elevating us into His presence, preparing us for what lies ahead. Glory to God for revelation! There are levels and steps that we just can't skip over to go somewhere else. The word tells us that we are made in God's image, and the LORD orders our steps. It is our trust in Him that directs our path, guiding us to our destined future.

Since God's ways and thoughts are higher than ours, He is in control. With every elevation, there are levels and steps we must pass and complete before reaching new dimensions. Just as a plane doesn't reach its highest altitude in one step, our spiritual journey involves phases that propel us to higher heights and depths. It's our unwavering trust in God's plan, our steadfast confidence in His guidance, that ensures we reach our destination.

We must get into the birthing position, preparing to be presented faultless for the glory of the Lord. We go through the trimesters of life waiting for the promises of God to manifest. When preparing to be birthed, one must first be put in the cephalic position where the fetus is head down and ready to enter the birth canal. The many obstacles and barriers must be dilated and removed, creating a clear path for one to follow. When we reach that last trimester, the head is crowning. It is at this moment God makes us a little lower than the heavenly beings and crowns us with glory and honor. He gives us dominion over the works of His hands, putting all things under our feet.

When we go through Divine Acceleration, we are walking it out by faith, carrying our spiritual babies until full term. Just like there is help to deliver natural babies, as our callings, we need the assistance of spiritual midwives, whether it is an Evangelist, Apostle, Therapist, Coach, Minister, and/or Pastor. David wrote, "Yet you brought me out of the womb; you made me trust in you, even at my mother's breast"-Psalm 22:9. God created us within the womb and became our midwife, presenting us as a special gift wrapped in purpose to the world. When God created us, He planted seeds of purpose within us that were predestined for the world. God placed everything inside of us, and we only need to push to birth all of it out in its season.

Once we have encamped about our world with our divine attitude, we have a greater capacity to handle more, increase our dependency and trust in God, and desire to please God first. As we divinely ascend, what we used to magnify becomes smaller, and what we thought was far off becomes a living, breathing reality. We see more clearly and taste the difference between milk and manna. When you reach divine elevation, it is now time for strong meat. We begin to appreciate all the things we used to run from because we did not want to change. We begin to see root causes instead of focusing on the band-aid of a problem. Finally, we begin to appreciate our embrace of present afflictions and become welcoming to what was once unfamiliar in our divine ascension!

As we continue this segment into divine ascension, we realize it's not a formula. It is a pattern laid out from the foundations of this world. It is to understand that each functioning worker in our flight to ascension may not resemble what we see on our television, but the workers that are assigned to us during our ascension are truly sent by God and forthcoming of any loose ends we may have missed! As we go up, the old us die, old habits become detestable, we hate the things we used to love, things that used to haunt us become our allies, and the hurt we used to have becomes our stepping stool. Oh, and the friends we used to treasure the most truly become ingrafted or completely fall off. We begin to show forth the character (or individual qualities of God) and attributes of God (or overall character of God).

Let us discuss humility for a moment. Humility is often misunderstood, especially in a world that sometimes equates it with weakness or subservience. True humility is about valuing oneself accurately and understanding one's place in the grander scheme of things. It involves recognizing one's strengths and weaknesses without misrepresenting them. Humility is rooted in a deep sense of self-awareness and respect, both for oneself and for others. It is not about making oneself small or insignificant; rather, it is about having a balanced view of one's abilities and contributions.

False humility, on the other hand, is a deceptive form of modesty that can be harmful. It often involves flattery and masked pridefulness, where individuals downplay their achievements or qualities in a way that seeks validation or praise from others. This can also include devaluing oneself to elevate someone else, which might seem noble on the surface but can lead to detrimental effects on one's self-esteem and mental well-being. Over time, such behaviors can erode a person's sense of self-worth and authenticity, leading to inner conflicts and even spiritual turmoil.

Engaging in false humility can open the door to spiritual warfare, as it creates an internal dissonance that can be exploited. It distracts from genuine self-improvement and spiritual growth by focusing on external validation rather than internal truth. Authentic humility, by contrast, fosters a sincere reverence unto God, placing divine honor above self-interest. It encourages a genuine respect for others and oneself, promoting a healthy and balanced perspective that is conducive to personal and spiritual well-being. Thus, embracing true humility is not only beneficial for personal development but also essential for maintaining spiritual harmony.

As we reach for the unknown, let us remain grounded in hope and faith while remaining humble, understanding it's not by our own actions or our own hand but truly an act of love from our Heavenly Father.

A FLIGHT TO A THREE-DIMENSIONAL LEGACY

We cannot Dethrone God's Process

Congratulations on reaching cruising altitude in your spiritual journey! As you ascend, it's crucial to secure your shield of faith and lace up the shoes of peace. These spiritual armaments will protect you as you navigate through a world where not everyone may celebrate your commitment to serve God with clean hands and a pure heart. The shield combined with the breastplate of righteousness and the helmet of salvation will guard your mind, heart, and body against the adversities that may arise, especially when the forces of darkness are unleashed against you for your divine dedication. Remember, God's armies raise a standard that no enemy can overcome, ensuring that you stay protected and victorious, as He has never lost a battle.

Commitment is key to ascending successfully into new realms. Agreeing with God's divine plan and security policies is essential. Accepting God's full will and counsel will help you avoid the repetitiveness of the same lessons. Full submission to His process is necessary to move forward; without it, rebellion and stagnation are inevitable. As you journey through life, transitioning from the worldly system to the kingdom's system, know that you are supported by the King Himself, who is the wind beneath your wings.

In the Divine Acceleration phase of your journey, it's important to release excess weight, baggage, indifference, and prejudices. This will allow you to love and be loved more freely. Understanding your physical and mental limitations and modifying unhealthy perceptions of yourself are vital steps. Realizing that you are a rare commodity, you will begin to see the importance of following God's process rather than trying to control the narrative. By learning how to conduct yourself in various situations and dealing with different personalities, you will not only capture new opportunities but also maintain your pace in building a legacy. Divine Acceleration is a new way of life, marked by accepting God's vision and walking it out, even through painful situations, by His Spirit. Keep your spiritual seatbelt fastened and access your C.L.U.E.S. – Cleave to God,

Leave the crowd, Utilize wisdom, Expel negativity, and Seize opportunities. This time is precious, as it brings the repayment of your past kindness and generosity, fulfilling God's promise. *"Instead of shame and dishonor, we will enjoy a double share of honor. We will possess a double portion of prosperity in our land, and everlasting joy will be ours"* -Isaiah 61:7. God is allowing me to share a peek in my personal full circle from marketplace employment to kingdom work I do now as a flight attendant. Writing this book was God breathed, and life lived. Each word, each sentence, felt like a whisper from God guiding my hand and shaping my thoughts. The process was not merely about putting pen to paper. It was about channeling a deeper wisdom that transcends the mundane and touches the eternal. This book is a testament to the moments of clarity and inspiration that come when one opens one's heart and mind to the possibilities of divine intervention. This process positioned me for **God's Reveal In Time ("GRIT")**. GRIT is often described as a combination of passion and perseverance that drives individuals to achieve their long-term goals. It's the tenacity to keep pushing forward, even in the face of adversity and setbacks. In essence, GRIT is a profound concept that encapsulates the perseverance and passion needed to achieve long-term goals. When we talk about GRIT in the context of faith, it highlights the importance of trusting in God's timing and promises. This journey is often marked by moments of waiting and personal growth, where our obedience and steadfastness play crucial roles. It requires us to hold onto our faith and continue to act in accordance with God's Word, even when the fulfillment of His promises seems delayed.

GRIT involves a deep-seated resolve to stay committed to our spiritual path despite the challenges and uncertainties we may face. It means believing that God's timing is perfect and that He is always working for our good, even when we cannot see it immediately. This trust is not passive; it calls for active obedience and a willingness to align our actions with God's will. Through this process, we develop a stronger, more resilient faith, capable of withstanding the trials and tribulations of life.

Grit Work

What is Grit Work? It is the process where I have transitioned and shifted into a different type of career. This was the manifestation of an ancient promise from God. The many dreams I've had of traveling the world never amounted in my mind to being a flight attendant. However, I thank God for the opportunity to be one because it has helped me embrace a higher standard, a new walk, a new day. What I thought was a loss, such as my previous corporate career, the loss in traction, and the loss in finances, was a beautiful change and resulted in my current career springing from ancient promises that God brought full circle. It reminded me of the saying it's not how I start, but how I finish. It's not what happened to us. It is about how we respond.

Cultivating grit involves developing a growth mindset, where challenges are viewed as opportunities for learning rather than insurmountable obstacles. It requires setting clear, long-term goals and breaking them down into manageable steps, all while maintaining enthusiasm and motivation. Support from mentors, peers, and a supportive environment can also play a crucial role in fostering grit. Ultimately, grit is about embracing the journey, staying passionate about your pursuits, and never giving up, no matter how tough the road ahead may seem.

Prior to starting this journey of becoming a flight attendant, I felt like I was walking with a higher purpose, true independence, and inevitable power. But this experience made me come off my high horse and realize there was so much more than what I was already doing. It also screamed I could feel great in one setting and be nowhere close to my designated purpose. What I found is that it was just a glimpse of the core of what I am to be a part of. For years, I worked in many arenas that highlighted my talent and my skills, but it was not the true fulfillment of my spiritual gifts. After I got the revelation, I noticed that, just as I mentioned in the preface, I was fulfilled in my flesh, not in my spirit. I was still missing something. I still needed water that never ran out and was never tainted.

We all have various talents and skills, but neither our talents nor our skills always lead to us fully functioning in our destined promise. It is our spiritual gifts that lead us into our full destiny. Paul wrote,

> *There are different kinds of gifts, but the same Spirit distributes them. There are different kinds of service, but the same Lord. There are different kinds of work, but the same God is at work in all of them and in everyone. Now, to each one, the manifestation of the Spirit is given for the common good. To one there is given through the Spirit a message of wisdom, to another a message of knowledge by means of the same Spirit, to another faith by the same Spirit, to another gifts of healing by that one Spirit, to another miraculous powers, to another prophecy, to another distinguishing between spirits, to another speaking in different kinds of tongues, and to still another the interpretation of tongues. All these are the work of one and the same Spirit, and he distributes them to each one, just as he determines.* -1 Corinthians 12:4-11 NIV

Renowned for his wisdom, King Solomon famously said, "A man's gift makes room for him and brings him before a great men." King Solomon shines a light on the value and power of one's talents and abilities. An individual's unique skills and gifts can open doors to opportunities and elevate them to positions of influence and recognition. The phrase "makes room for him" implies that when a person diligently develops and utilizes their natural abilities, these talents can create opportunities that otherwise might not be accessible. It underscores the idea that competence and excellence in one's craft can lead to greater visibility and acknowledgment, often paving the way to interact with influential and powerful individuals. God has called us to nurture and harness one's talents, and they hold the potential to impact one's trajectory in life significantly.

Personal growth and success are not solely dependent on external factors like social status or wealth but rather on the intrinsic qualities and gifts that one brings to the table. By recognizing and honing these gifts, one can gain a sense of clear direction aligning with the plans God has in place for one's life. One's unique abilities have the power to create opportunities and shape our destinies.

On the road to divine acceleration, we must leave what we have not been called to redeem and accept the assignments we have been given without hesitations and reservations. Let us learn that part of growing up is respecting ourselves and others! Let's learn how to stay focused and stay on task daily. The Grit work breaks down the unhealthy coping mechanisms to replace them with healthy coping mechanisms. As a result, the Grit works as we accelerate; we remove all the guilty inconsistencies as we grow in favor and stature with God and man.

During Divine Acceleration, we must closely monitor our conversations and the company we keep. The company we keep can hinder our rate of momentum on many levels, adding barriers to our mind, will, and intellect (our soul). We should consistently converse and interact with those who have genuine love, concern, and compassion for us, not focusing on what we can get from each other or asking each other what we bring to the table. I've learned that divine acceleration moments are made available to those who are willing to encourage, guide, build, and edify (meaning instruct and improve) others. Sometimes, we miss out on our queues to pivot forward due to selfish motives or unwillingness to change our perception (mindset). Until we yield, we will remain in a constant cycle, repeating things we never wanted to experience again. We must die to self to build others and walk in His divine assembly. King Solomon further writes, *"Just as a body, though one, has many parts, but all its many parts form one body, so it is with Christ"*-1 Corinthians 12:12 NIV. There is no I in oneness. Though there are many gifts, they are joined together to work together collectively to accomplish the mission of Christ. Getting to a level of acceleration requires one's mindset to be of a team and not of oneself.

A few key signs illuminate us as we walk into divine acceleration. One is that we enter a season of divine wisdom, understanding, and fruit. Two is that our inner circle changes rapidly and drastically, and three our whole outlook on life begins to shift up. Opportunities that were once unreachable become available. Although I sensed I was to be a flight attendant years ago, it wasn't until the assigned people were released and within the appointed time that I realized I was. I first had to walk in forgiveness and mercy, which positioned me to be released into my recovery and redemption position, where I was able to discuss my grit work challenges without being offended. According to Galatians 1, we harvest what we plant. Now, I can help my neighbor, and I learned this keeps me from falling into the same temptation. It also shows how to decrease the fate of depressurization issues on others by ensuring my cabin (mind) is filled and sealed with the Holy Spirit.

Divine acceleration also involves mentally accepting and understanding who you are. It's about writing and living the vision on purpose, walking it out each minute, hour, and day. Walking is to proceed by steps and/or to march. If God said it, do it, endure it, build it; it will work out for your good. Let us live as our purposes unfold, releasing our inherent power to evolve and be a part of others' evolution each time we step in obedience.

I have always wanted to be a flight attendant ever since I was a teen, about 16. However, the qualifications and steps to achieve it were different than today. I ended up being a part of a scam as I paid to go to flight attendant training. Those of you who know aviation are probably floored right now, LOL. The definitive confirmation of the scam is they took my money, and after completing all the assignments and tests, they advised me that I did not meet the weight qualifications to serve as an airline stewardess (flight attendant). After this failure, or at least I thought, I encouraged myself to build new aspirations, new goals, better goals, I thought, never physically looking back. While I was a little stuck in rage and disappointment mentally, I let my standards go because I lacked understanding and wisdom. See, we can be disappointed, but don't stay there as it ends up being a literal viral infection of our view of hope and faith. I found that God will show us a glimpse of where we are going, but it does not mean it is about to happen at the time when he shows us.

I began drinking heavily, amongst other things, until I matured enough to realize my life and purpose were more important than sitting in a soap box of sin, weights, misunderstandings, miscommunications, lack of self-awareness, and disrespect. That season was not the safest or greatest period of my life. I went from healthy to unhealthy in my spirit. I attempted to drown my misunderstanding of the denial. This is why we must know the voice that speaks to us and be able to process soberly through situations that upset us so we will not be misguided in our thinking or perception of who we still are, regardless of the delays. We must gain the understanding that delay does not mean denied. The wisdom of King Solomon made us aware of the timing of God in the book of Ecclesiastes, as there is a time and a place for everything. At times, we truly are not yet prepared for what we think we are ready for. But if we begin to understand and walk in faith, GOD will take ten steps in demonstration to highlight the abundant path. He is not the author of confusion and makes plain the plans He has for our lives. It's our choice to seek Him to reveal these plans to us. In the acceleration process, you will find yourself seeking and thirsting for Him more and more as you enter an unfamiliar place that requires the assistance of the navigation system to get around. He desires us to take Him at His Word and apply it to our daily walk through life. His divine response to our faith is not just equal to our efforts but magnified many times. Each step taken is met with an even greater display of God's divine presence and love. When I ignored my emotions and pushed past me, I crossed over into new opportunities and dimensions. Emotions can trap you and make you feel unqualified, unprepared, and unproductive. Emotions can make you feel inadequate for your call. Overriding our emotions equips us to fulfill the roles we are to be assigned. Pushing into new levels of dimensions took me eating the fruit of self-control and change my perception of myself. Looking in the mirror, I had to see beyond my flesh and look deep within my Spirit at who God called me to be. No longer did

I see I, but I saw the seal of God on my life. I had been leveling up for years but never crossing over into higher dimensions. It wasn't until I became one with God and took ownership of all He has planted within me that I was ready for higher dimensions. Luke, the evangelist, says, *"To whom much is given, much is required"* -Luke 12:48. I had to become the student again and remain in a student's mindset to become more knowledgeable of my gifts. I realized that where I was trying to get to on my own, God had already put me there; I just had to be developed. Apostle Paul said it best, *"And God raised us up with Christ and seated us with him in the heavenly realms in Christ Jesus…"* -Ephesians 2:6 NIV.

The Walk of Sobriety

"Be sober-minded; be watchful. Your adversary, the devil, prowls around like a roaring lion, seeking someone to devour." 1 Peter 5:8

Sobriety is calling our names!! Walking in Sobriety is more than being sober from alcohol and drugs. It's deeper than that. Walking in Sobriety is maintaining pure thinking, a good bill of health, and a clear mindset, forgiving ourselves and others, releasing all burdens, and casting all our cares unto the LORD.

Before I could even enter my double promise, I almost lost everything, including a corporate job that paid a good salary—specifically, the highest salary I've been paid. I was wrongfully let go, and I couldn't understand why. I felt like I was going through a Job experience. As time went on, I'm so glad the company representative fired me for performance. The job paid me one salary while I did three to four jobs daily! But flesh began to ask God why and how I could lose what He gave me. I soon realized it was the breaking into divine acceleration by assuming this much responsibility. The job I lost was just my launching pad into greater beginnings. When you're in a place of trusting God, it's no longer about the tangible finances. Granted, money does solve problems. However, God wants to know if you will trust Him to supply all of your needs. Our work for the kingdom will override the need for physical money. For the Lord is our shepherd, we shall not want. (Psalms 23) When we step into purpose, greater resources shall follow through our obedience. Purpose restores us better than carnal positions we may mistake as God's plan. God can use opportunities to set us up for more than the obvious landing.

    He destined my career to flourish and activate His visions and desires. My walk of sobriety started when I allowed the Holy Spirit to enlighten my understanding of His divine timing. I went through a couple of airlines showing up as my representative, but when I applied for my current airline, my whole mindset shifted, and my understanding synced with God's grace and plans for my life. Revelation hit, "And the last shall be first." I went into my current airline with the remaining strength, just being myself and settling in that I was enough. Guess what? When you just be yourself, good and great, things begin to open right before your eyes. When this airline opened its doors, the steps went smoothly. This is the same way you can see that your steps are being ordered. This formed an implication in my mind that it was meant for me. I began to move along with the process, pushing past the familiar, the familiar with which was trying to sabotage my divine flow and process. I went on to my scheduled interview with my current airline. At that moment, I had nothing to lose and everything to gain in my life; I had entered the newness of life! It finally dawned on me that this round was getting ready to be comprehensive and serious. This was God's hand bringing me FULL CIRCLE! This full-circle revelation and impartation didn't fully hit my spirit until it became an active demonstration when I looked up. I was still present at the interview process after several hours. What was once a dream started to become a reality. It helped me to realize that divine acceleration periods can never be forced; they are at an appointed time for taxi, take-off, and landing. After enough of the ferry flights, I was walking to my appointment with Destiny. During this time of newness, I had just come into full sobriety of what I was to be doing.

A FLIGHT TO A THREE-DIMENSIONAL LEGACY

Walking sincerely sober teaches you to accept yourself and who you are in God. In divine acceleration, we must walk in sobriety, watching the adversary and not allowing him to creep into unhealed crevices and cracks within our minds, will, and intellect. This way, we can enter new levels of favor and grace. We tend to find another level of acceleration and favor when we decide to please the LORD. God stirs us up while we continue to read the word. These deposits are slowly released as we are found faithful and commendable. As we divinely ascend, we will find that there are more and more people who do not have a genuine heart in mind; they may be nosey. These people tend to cast shade on you in front of the crowd to make light of their insecurities or for personal reasons. But I admonish you to stand firm, and they will flee. This means we should build a community of trustworthy people so we won't be dependent on fake people to share oxygen with us or help themselves out and drop us as we ascend. This also means that we may have taken a joke in one season but understand that the same joke happening during the divine acceleration period is a hindrance and backlash of the adversary working through everyday folks. For example, while entering the line as a flight attendant, there were a few distractions in front of customers during the flight. But because I was unbothered, I let it roll off my back and gave it over to God.

Our priority and choice should be ensuring we have a trustworthy circle and/or network. A circle that will intercede for you instead of talking about you or your problems. A circle that prays for those who persecuted them. A circle that will not hinder you from doing your jobs and/or work effectively. Additionally, we must remain calm during divine acceleration, not allowing others to move our needle of mercy, grace, and peace. Even when the days are really hard, find a way to detox from people who try to steal your joy. If you experience this a lot, it could be indicative of you coming up and out of old things and into the NEW. This means many people see you're changing and becoming all you are created to be.

A FLIGHT TO A THREE-DIMENSIONAL LEGACY

When experiencing many public challenges, think of Jesus and how people would try to reduce who he was to better suit their own perception of him, not realizing that he is all God in the flesh, who died for all our sins, gave up the ghost on his own, and dynamically rose the third day with all power and keys of death and hades in his hands. There are days during divine acceleration when people will try to capitalize on your human flaws, but remember, you will win, and not one weapon will prosper. I speak over those reading this book right now, A thousand may fall at your side, ten thousand at your right hand, but it will not come near you (Psalms 91:7) in the name of Jesus.

In divine acceleration, I learned that a level and a dimension are different. I wouldn't have known about dimensions if I hadn't let the familiar and inevitable levels go. Oxford languages define a level as a horizontal plane or line with respect to the distance above or below a given point; make equal or similar. In contrast, a dimension is defined as vast, greatness, depth, or size. I also look at dimension as being God's will. God is very specific when he lists the dimensions when it comes to building people and structures.

Walking in Divine Acceleration will increase our mental capacity to write the vision and make it plain, which can be called the blueprint. A blueprint is our identity and is in God and given by God, our creator. Our identity is within Him, and the blueprint will reveal who we are, what we are supposed to be doing, and where we are supposed to go. When we enter new dimensions, our level of understanding is not the same as in previous dimensions. We may feel a tearing sensation, not physically, but a detox of prior experiences that we have been through as we enter new places, unfamiliar places. When entering new places, we must gain an understanding of balance. We must **B**elieve **A**lways, **L**etting **A**ll **N**eeded **C**omfort **E**merge ("**BALANCE**").

Balance becomes like nourishment, and without it, we will soon run dry. There is a need to balance schedules, outings, meetings, FaceTime, Zoom, Family, work, and other roles. Otherwise, one can find themselves always feeling overwhelmed, depleted, and weighed down. Balance brings forth healthy boundaries to one's life. The best way to balance is to seek God for your daily agenda and remember that everything does not have to be done all in one day. Prioritize and compartmentalize your responsibilities as you are led by the Spirit.

Balance is often misconceived as an equal distribution of time, energy, and resources across all areas of life. However, true balance is more about finding a harmonious arrangement that aligns with your personal values, priorities, and circumstances. It's about recognizing that different aspects of life demand varying degrees of attention at different times and being flexible enough to adapt to those needs without feeling overwhelmed or guilty. Achieving balance means understanding that some areas may take precedence over others depending on your current goals and situations. Balance includes frequent exercising, staying focused, not defaulting to being a victim, loving yourself, loving others, genuinely cutting ties with people that may hold us back from excelling. The key is to remain mindful of these shifts and make conscious decisions that reflect your evolving priorities. Furthermore, balance involves setting realistic expectations and boundaries. It requires recognizing your limits and being kind to yourself when you cannot give equal attention to everything. By practicing self-awareness and self-compassion, you can navigate through the flow of life's demands more gracefully. Ultimately, balance is not about achieving a perfect equilibrium but creating a fulfilling and sustainable way of living that allows you to thrive in all facets of life. This determines whether you can fully enter in divine acceleration. Apostle Paul said, *"God has apportioned to each a degree of faith and a purpose designed for service"* -Romans 12:3 AMP

Sometimes, people we've been around most of our lives, including family, may have deterred us from making it to our promise. We must evaluate our surroundings and adjust our ailerons and your leading-edge slats as we transition from area to area. You might have to downshift and switch to a lower landing gear (being humble) to process instead of staying at the same momentum if you put a written end date so you don't lose momentum. Sure, everyone needs a break, so we must make sure we're taking care of ourselves properly in the midst of this. We want to live to see what we work so hard to build, so there must be balance.

As we learn how to process situations, we come to a point where we don't quite remember the pain of our past experiences. God positions us to feel the greatest glory encounter of our lives, and his word confirms this to be true. Apostle Paul said, *"For I reckon that the sufferings of this present time are not worthy to be compared with the glory which shall be revealed in us"* – Romans 8:18 KJV. God will make us forget our pain and accept His Joy, and all that tried to hinder us will be washed away in the sea of forgetfulness. In these moments, trust God's release and don't complain lest we get beside ourselves and delay our blessings. If we complain too much, that's not a good place. Don't get so tired that we strike the opportunities like Moses instead of speaking to the opportunities after being given specific instructions. Job 11:16 NLT says, *"You will forget your misery; it will be like water flowing away."* Now, let us go up together to the call to the mount!

A Call to the Mount

Despite what happens, happening, or happened, Beloved, there is a call on your life that you will answer. Even when something is being killed from one of our perspectives while something is being birthed, which is thriving on the other end of our lives, still, we must stand the test, the test to conquer division (God's will and our emotions) and derision (verbal abuse). It is a call, not a message, not a tweet, not a tag; it is not a shout-out, the call, the ascension is personal. Socially, we reflect on how we lack the human touch more and more. We interact with machines, automated tellers, virtual chat, and digital chat. We are talking about being touched through the love of God, who formed us from the dust of the earth. Yes, the call is from the one John the Baptist who tells us we are not worthy to tie his shoes (Jesus). Still, God called us even after his calculations of us, after the shame of rejections, after the walking ahead of him and us having to be knocked back on track, he still called us to walk out what he has given us/ you, that no one, but you/I, can carry it out. God's call comes with clear instructions and directions. No, we are not perfect; you heard me, WE are not perfect, but this is what qualifies us in the development of the true ministry. You have to go through a lot of steps to answer the call. As we answer our calls, there is an expected end for us, and we all have been assigned to assist, nurture, and impart.

Either we fight to maintain our growth mindset to keep winning in spirit first, before the physical, or we will get swallowed up in one bite. Life is often viewed as a game of chess, you see. We prophesy in part, and so the part that we are not privy to is what tests us to ensure we demonstrate integrity, grit, and power to carry the call. See, we can all pick up the phone and say yes across the live wire, online video, and or conference call, but where are we? Where are we really when the rubber meets the road? We get a little fickle; we are just talking. But when we get the call from the Lord, we may not know that it is him at first if we are not regularly communing with him, circumcising our eyes and ears consistently.

Part of the call opens up divine ascension results, partially based on how our level of gratitude in our attitude is /was during each delay, during each revamp, during each reroute, during each revelation, during each reconstruction, and during each encounter. Are we living in the present, utilizing the gifts we have been given to walk through moments that we have been entrusted with? When you are present and you lead by example, you are setting others free through your obedience, showing them how important it is to be present in each moment as instructions are given during the answering of our call. King Solomon wrote, "For in much human wisdom there is much displeasure and exasperation, increasing knowledge increases sorrow" – Ecclesiastes 1:18 AMP. I felt this in a recent conversation with a family that experienced a fire in their home. I was glad to know, but there was much grief and more expansion of wisdom on handling things. As people gain more wisdom, they become more aware of the imperfections and injustices in the world. Solomon highlights the paradox that while wisdom is valuable and sought after, it can also bring about a more profound sense of sorrow as one becomes more attuned to the harsh realities of life. Solomon's statement serves as a reminder of the importance of humility and balance in pursuing knowledge. It suggests that wisdom should be tempered with understanding its potential burdens and accepting the things that cannot be changed. King Solomon's words encourage a reflective approach to life, where the pursuit of wisdom is balanced with recognizing its accompanying challenges.

Congratulations on Accelerating!!! As we journey through life, we encounter myriad challenges and triumphs. The Bible is our manuscript and source of wisdom and guidance that offers profound insights that can help us navigate these experiences. Isaiah 40:31 states, "But those who wait on the Lord shall have renewed strength. They will soar on wings like eagles; they will run and not grow weary; they will walk and not be faint." This passage serves as a reminder that placing our faith in a higher power can provide us with the strength and resilience needed to overcome obstacles and continue our journey with renewed vigor and purpose.

In moments of doubt or adversity, it is essential to remember the promises of hope and perseverance found within the scriptures. Jeremiah 29:11 tells us that God knows the plans he has for us. He even knows the thoughts he thinks towards us—plans to prosper us and not to harm us, plans and thoughts to give us hope and a future. It encourages us to trust this plan, even when the path seems uncertain or daunting.

By internalizing these messages and allowing them to influence our thoughts and actions, we can find the strength to overcome any challenge and embrace the future with confidence and optimism. Let these timeless words be a beacon of light, illuminating our path and reminding us that we are never alone in our journey.

Divine Acceleration Discussion

1. How do you interpret the concept of divine acceleration in your personal spiritual journey, and what experiences have shaped this understanding for you?

   _____

   _____

   _____

   _____

   _____

   _____

   _____

2. Can you share a story or an example from your life or someone you know where divine acceleration was evident, and what impact did it have on their faith?

   _____

   _____

   _____

   _____

   _____

   _____

   _____

3. What role does prayer and faith play in inviting or recognizing divine acceleration in your life?

_____

_____

_____

_____

_____

_____

4. How can one prepare themselves spiritually and mentally to receive and handle divine acceleration when it occurs?

_____

_____

_____

_____

_____

_____

_____

5. What are some scriptures or teachings that you find particularly relevant to understanding divine acceleration?

_____

_____

_____

_____

_____

_____

_____

6. How do you balance the idea of divine acceleration with the concept of patience and waiting on God's timing?

_____

_____

_____

_____

_____

_____

_____

7. In times of waiting or delay, how do you maintain hope and faith in the possibility of divine acceleration?

_____

_____

_____

_____

_____

_____

_____

8. What advice would you give to someone who feels stuck or is seeking divine acceleration in their life but is unsure where to start?

_____

_____

_____

_____

_____

_____

_____

ABOUT THE AUTHOR

Vanessa Brown has a plethora of skills and opportunities and consistent customer service knowledge of over 30 years. She is an empty nester and the mother of two young adult children, Ceion (a boy) and Ceona (a girl). She lives in Arlington, TX. In 2019, she co-authored her first writing with many other authors. Her feature was in Chapter 3, titled "The Inseparable Sustainer," in the Woman of Purpose book published by Higgins Publishing Company.

The Holy Spirit revealed that she had been teaching and mindset coaching individuals and groups for years. As a result, Vanessa Brown Global, LLC, was formed in 2023. Her LLC vision extends her vision as an author, mindset coach, product reviewer, model, and global ministry leader.

A FLIGHT TO A THREE-DIMENSIONAL LEGACY

She works as a Public Relations Manager and oversees the Social Media team for Empower Me Global Ministries as the face of the company. Empower Me Global Ministries and Living Waters Global Publishing was founded by Prophetess Aleshia Brown.

When we make up our minds that the just shall live by faith, God has now called us upon the water. I pray that your hearts will be flooded with light so that you can understand the confident hope he has given to those he called—his holy people who are his rich and glorious inheritance.

Being a flight attendant taught me that I don't have to live a limited life. It taught me to pay attention to details and how operations in my life go toward where I am going and not where I am. Being a flight attendant also taught me to love others, cultures, and the nationalities of people. It taught me to take courage by the palm of my hand, compress it, release it, and build it. Almost like the scripture says, "pressed down, shaking together, and running over!" The knowledge I have gained from being a flight attendant has changed the trajectory of my perception and my walk of life.

You can follow this author via Facebook, Instagram, and LinkedIn @VanessaBrownGlobal

For TikTok & YouTube @MindsetCoachV

If you would like to book her as a guest speaker, you can send information to vanessabrownglobal@gmail.com, or you can visit her website at https://vanessabrownglobal.org/mindsetcoachv